NICHOLSON

CENTRAL STREETFINDER

CW00405207

Central London Streetfinder
© Robert Nicholson Publications Limited
1987
First published 1986
Second edition 1987

Based upon the Ordnance Survey Map
with the sanction of the Controller of Her
Majesty's Stationery Office. Crown
Copyright reserved.

Original design Robert Nicholson and
Romek Marber.

London Guide tourist information
© Robert Nicholson Publications Limited
1987

All other maps
© Robert Nicholson Publications Limited
1987

London Underground map by kind
permission of London Transport.

Published and distributed by
Robert Nicholson Publications Ltd
16 Golden Square
London W1R 4BN

Great care has been taken throughout
this book to be accurate but the
publishers cannot accept responsibility
for any errors which appear, or their
consequences.

Printed in Great Britain by
John Bartholomew and Son Ltd
Edinburgh

ISBN 0 94 857605 7
86/2/240

Symbols

†	Church
✚	Hospital
🚗	Car park
🏛	Historic buildings
🏚	Small buildings
☗	Schools
▬	Sports stadium
⊖	London Underground station
✎	British Rail station
🎮	Coach station
✈	Air terminal
⇌	British Rail terminal
PO	Post office
Pol	Police station
⟶	One ways
⋯⋯	Footpath
⚞	Thames Water Authority piers
50 ▶ ◀ 100	Figure indicating the direction of street numbering and the approximate position
▦	Park, Golf course, Sports field, Recreation ground, Garden
▦	Cemetery, Allotment, Heath, Down, Open space

Large scale   Central area

	½ mile
	½ km

ROBERT NICHOLSON PUBLICATIONS

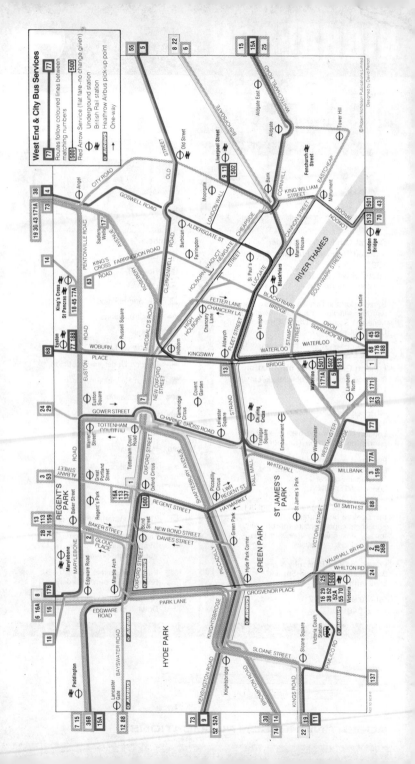

West End & City Bus Services

Routes follow coloured lines between matching numbers

Red Arrow Service (flat fare –no change given)

⊖ Underground station

≒ British Rail station

⊕ AIRBUS Heathrow Airbus pick-up point

↑ One-way

© Robert Nicholson Publications Limited

Designed by David Perrott

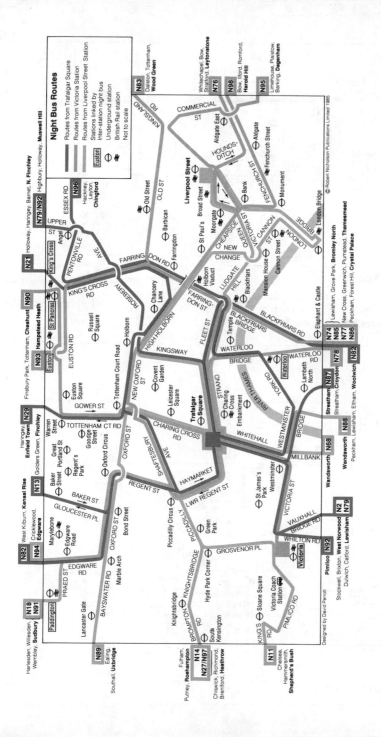

Night Bus Routes

Routes from Trafalgar Square
Routes from Victoria Station
Routes from Liverpool Street Station
Stations linked by inter-station night bus
⊖ Underground station
⇄ British Rail station
Not to scale

Euston British Rail station

© Robert Nicholson Publications Limited 1985

Designed by David Perrott

N18 N91 Harlesden, Willesden, Wembley, **Sudbury**

N82 West Kilburn, **Kensal Rise**
N94 Cricklewood, **Edgware**

N13 Golders Green, **Finchley**

N29 Haringey, **Enfield Town**

Euston **N93** Hampstead Heath

St Pancras **N90** Finsbury Park, Tottenham, **Cheshunt**

King's Cross **N2** Holloway, Haringey, Barnet, **N. Finchley**

N79/N92 Highbury, Holloway, **Muswell Hill**

ESSEX RD **N96** Hackney, Leyton, **Chingford**

N83 Dalston, Tottenham, **Wood Green**

N76 Whitechapel, Bow, Stratford, **Leytonstone**

N98 Bow, Ilford, Romford, **Harold Hill**

N95 Limehouse, Plaistow, Barking, **Degenham**

N89 Ealing, Southall, **Uxbridge**

N14 Fulham, Putney, **Roehampton**
N27/N97 Chiswick, Richmond, Brentford, **Heathrow**

N11 Chelsea, Hammersmith, **Shepherd's Bush**

Pimlico **N92** Stockwell, Brixton, West Norwood, **Lewisham**
N2 N79 Dulwich, Catford, **Lewisham**

Victoria

Wandsworth **N68** Peckham, Lewisham, Eltham, **Woolwich**

N88 Wandsworth

Streatham **N87** Streatham, **Croydon**

N78 **N82** Waterloo

N74 N85 N77 N86 Lewisham, Grove Park, **Bromley North** / New Cross, Greenwich, Plumstead, **Thamesmead** / Peckham, Forest Hill, **Crystal Palace**

Elephant & Castle

London Bridge

Liverpool Street

Aldgate East / Aldgate / Fenchurch Street / Monument / Bank / Broad Street

Old Street / Barbican / Farringdon / St Paul's / Moorgate / Cannon Street / Mansion House / Blackfriars / Temple / Holborn Viaduct / Ludgate Hill

Chancery Lane / Holborn / Russell Square

Euston Square / Warren Street / Goodge Street / Tottenham Court Road / Oxford Circus

Baker Street / Great Portland Street / Regent's Park / Edgware Road / Marylebone / Bond Street

Lancaster Gate / Marble Arch / Paddington

Hyde Park Corner / Knightsbridge / South Kensington / Sloane Square / Victoria Coach Station

Green Park / Piccadilly Circus / St James's Park / Charing Cross / Leicester Square / Covent Garden / Trafalgar Square

Westminster / Waterloo / Lambeth North / Vauxhall

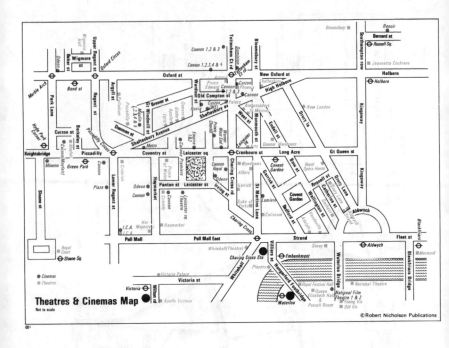

Theatres & Cinemas Map

Not to scale

● Cinemas
■ Theatres

©Robert Nicholson Publications

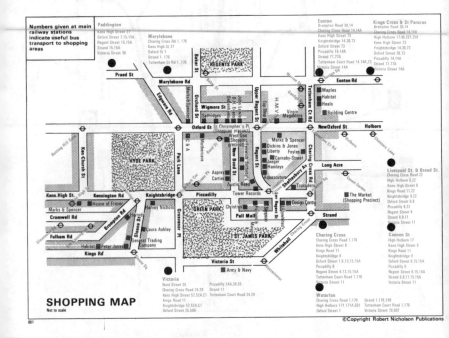

SHOPPING MAP

Not to scale

Numbers given at main railway stations indicate useful bus transport to shopping areas

Paddington
Kens High Street 27
Oxford Street 7,15,15A
Regent Street 15,15A
Strand 15,15A
Victoria Street 36

Marylebone
Charing Cross Rd 1, 176
Kens High St 27
Oxford St 1
Strand 1, 176
Tottenham Ct Rd 1, 176

Euston
Brompton Road 30,14
Charing Cross Road 14,14A
Kens High Street 73
Knightsbridge 14,30,73
Oxford Street 73
Piccadilly 14,14A
Strand 77,77A
Tottenham Court Road 14,14A,73
Victoria 14A

Kings Cross & St Pancras
Brompton Road 30,14
Charing Cross Road 14,14A
High Holborn 17,45,221,259
Kens High Street 73
Knightsbridge 14,30,73
Oxford Street 30,73
Piccadilly 14,14A
Strand 77,77A
Victoria Street 14A

Kens.High St.
Kensington Rd
Cromwell Rd
Fulham Rd
Kings Rd

Liverpool St.& Broad St.
Charing Cross Road 22
High Holborn 8,22
Kens High Street 8
Kings Road 11,22
Knightsbridge 9,22
Piccadilly 9,22
Regent Street 8
Strand 6,9,11
Victoria Street 11

Cannon St
High Holborn 17
Kens High Street 9
Kings Road 11
Knightsbridge 9
Oxford Street 8,15,15A
Piccadilly 9
Regent Street 8,15,15A
Strand 6,9,11,15,15A
Victoria Street 11

Charing Cross
Charing Cross Road 1,176
Kens High Street 9
Kings Road 11
Knightsbridge 9
Oxford Street 1,8,13,15,15A
Piccadilly 9
Regent Street 6,13,15,15A
Tottenham Court Road 1,176
Victoria Street 11

Victoria
Bond Street 25
Charing Cross Road 24,29
Kens High Street 52,52A,C1
Kings Road 11
Knightsbridge 52,52A,C1
Oxford Street 25,500

Piccadilly 14A,38,55
Strand 11
Tottenham Court Road 24,29

Waterloo
Charing Cross Road 1,176
High Holborn 171,171A,501
Oxford Street

Strand 1,176,199
Tottenham Court Road 1,176
Victoria Street 70,507

©Copyright Robert Nicholson Publications

KEY MAP

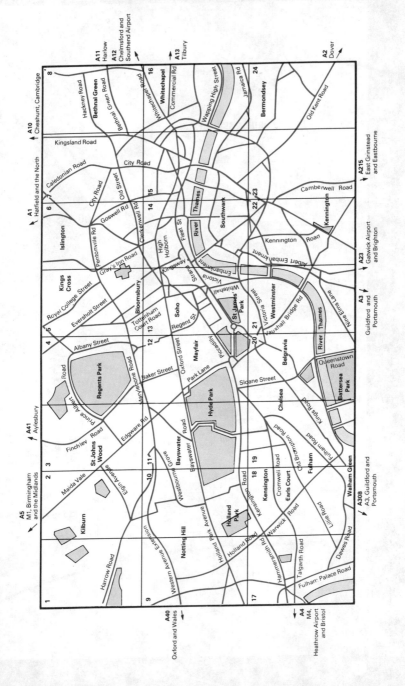

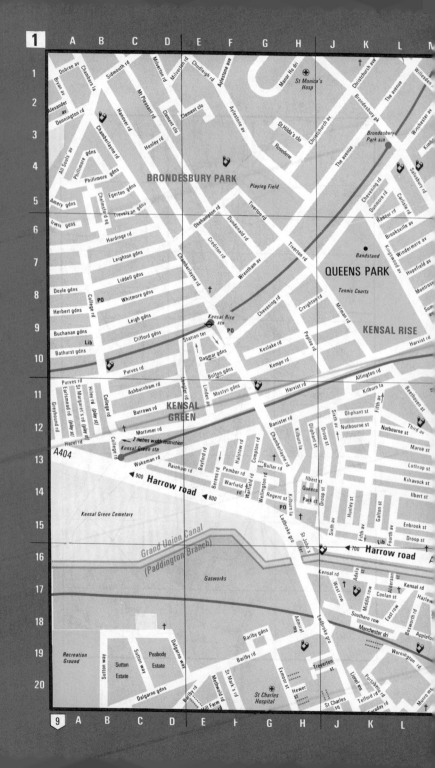

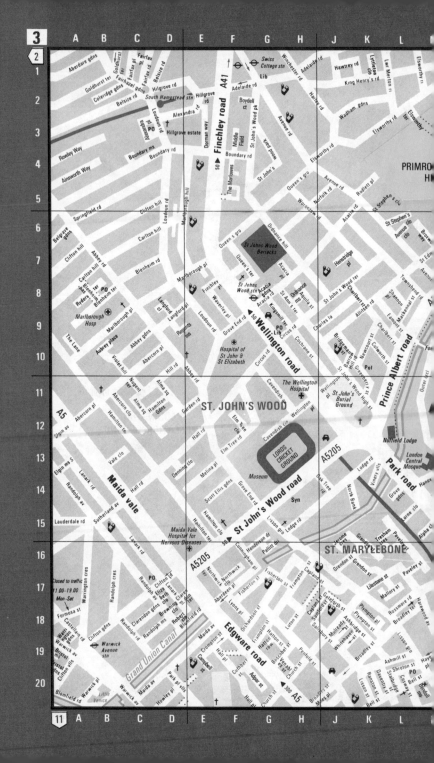

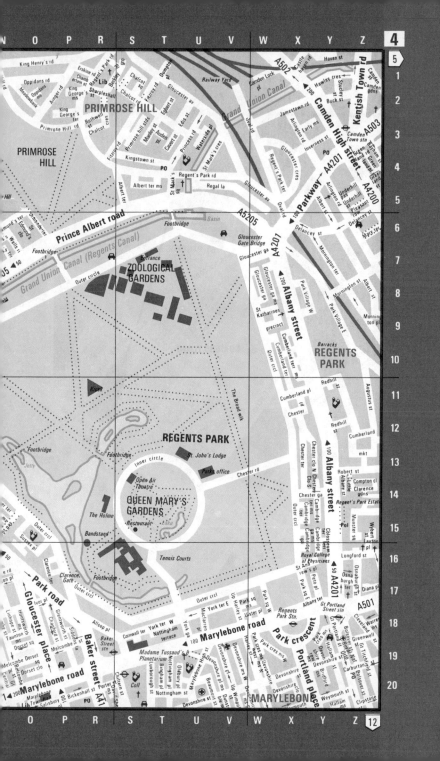

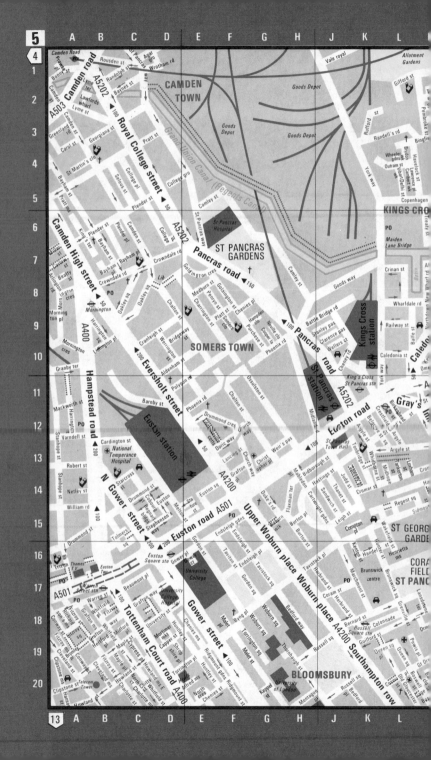

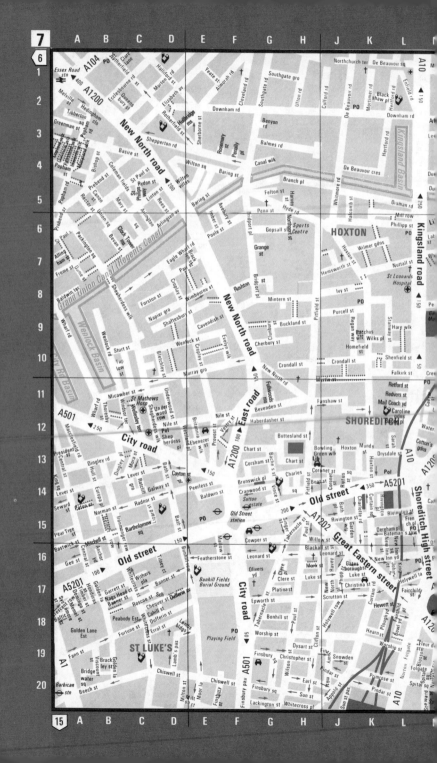

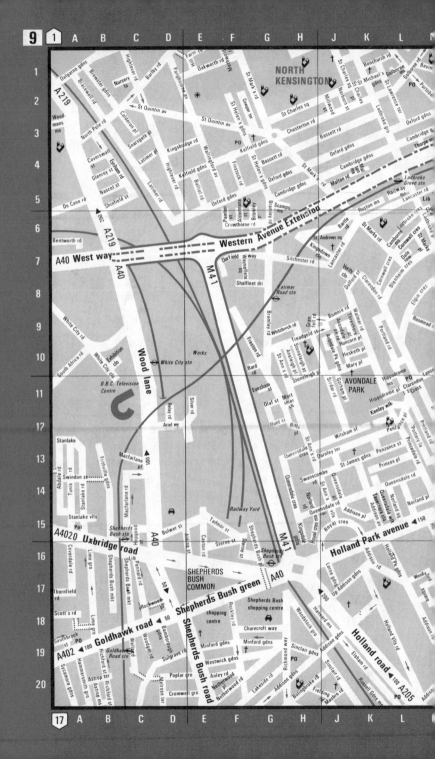

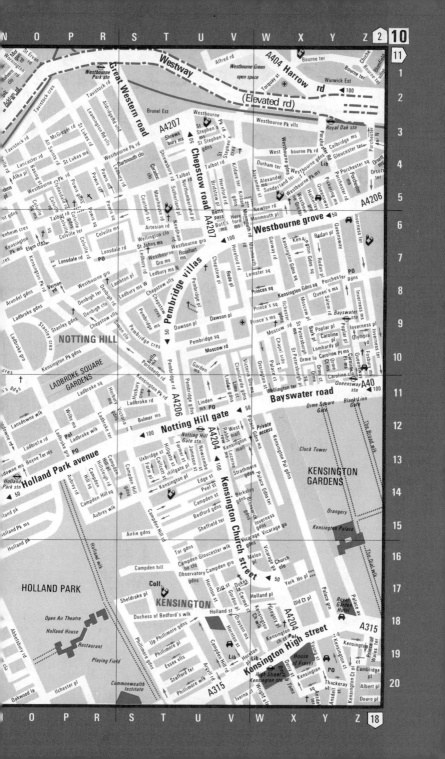

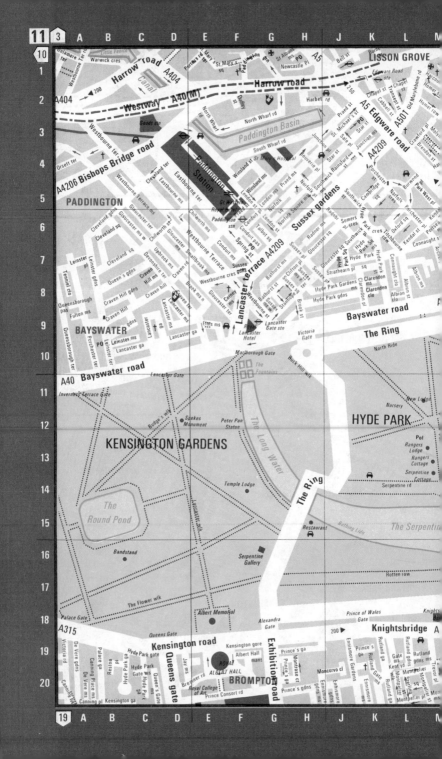

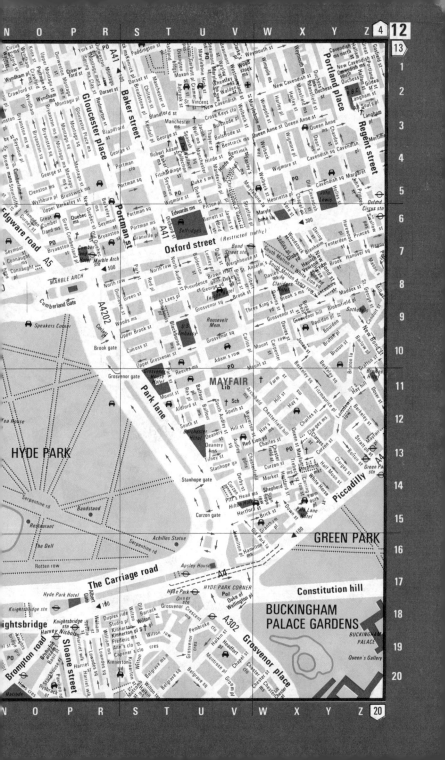

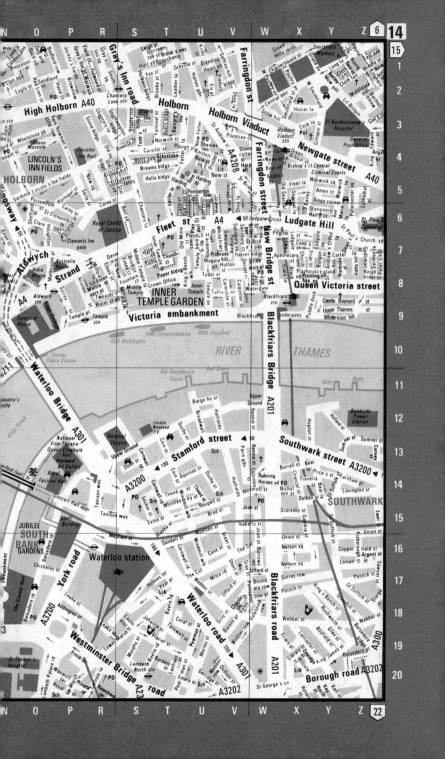

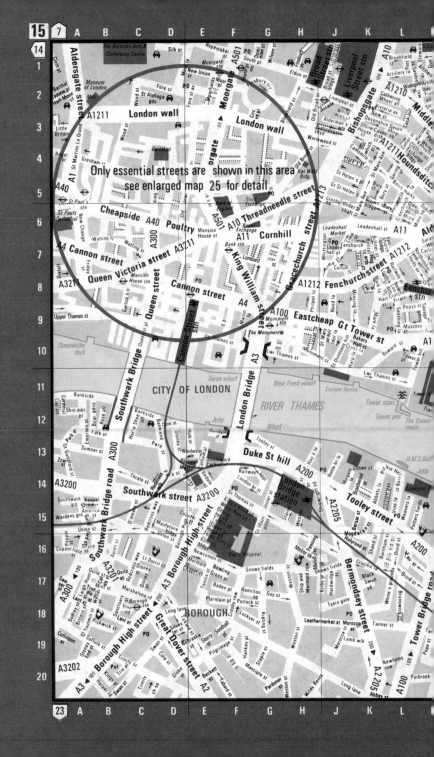

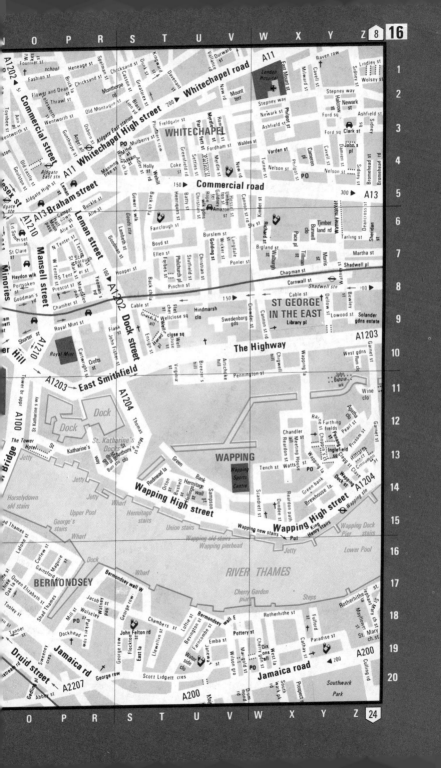

A B C D E F G H J K L M

1 2 3 4 5 6 7 8 9 10 11 12 13 14 15 16 17 18 19 20

Benbow rd
Beauclerc rd
Richford st
Sulgrave rd
Melrose gdns
Lakeside rd
Addison gdns
Bolingbroke rd
Irving rd
Holland rd
Sinclair rd
Russell gdns
A205
Holland gdns
Coulter rd
Osman rd
Batoum gdns
A219
Blythe
pl
Redan st
Masbro rd
Nisson rd
Ceylon rd
Porten rd
Russell
Hebron rd
Amor rd
Trussley rd
Grove ms
Lena gdns
Dewhurst rd
Blythe rd
Spring vale ter
Faroe rd
Grattan rd
Hazlitt ms
Kensingtn
(Olympia)
Marco rd
Agate rd
Sterndale rd
Augustine rd
Applegarth rd
Caithness rd
Coulter rd
Aynhoe rd
Maclise rd
Beaconsfield
Adie rd
Barb ms
Dunsany rd
Haarlem rd
Blythe
PO
Olympia
Shepherd's Bush road
Brook grn
BROOK GREEN
Brook grn
† Kilmarsh rd
Overstone rd
Shepherd's Bush tn
Brook grn
PO
Southerton rd
Hammersmith gro
Playing Field
BROOK GREEN
Brook grn
Blythe rd
50
Bishop King's
Hlley rd
Pol
Lib
Bute gdns
N End rd
Southcombe st
Cumberland
cres
A315 Glenthorne rd
Beadon road
Hammersmith stn
200
West London Hospital
Wolverton gdns
Rowan ter
Bute gdns
Rowan rd
Hammersmith road
Maunder rd
Edith rd
Vernon st
Vernon ms
Cambridge gro
Leamore st
Ashcroft sq
Hammersmith bdwy
A315
200
Colet gdns
More close
Fitz George av FitzJames
A315 King street
Hammersmith stn
Fareham ct.
Butterwick
Chalk hill rd
Shortlands
WEST KENSINGTON
Lily close
Edith rd
Down pl
Bridge av
Anger wlk
Black's rd
Bridge road
PO
Gt Church la
Coll
Gunterstone rd
Baron's keep
Glazbury rd
Gwendwr rd
Gt West rd
Hammersmith flyover
Talgarth road
Hammersmith
Bridge view
Rutland gro
Sussex pl
Wortidge st
Queen Caroline st
A219
PO
Barons Court stn
Baron's ct rd
Lower mall
Lower mall
River ter
Crisp rd
St James st
Chancellor's st
Fulham Palace road
Yeldham rd
Biscay rd
Margravine gdns
Hammersmith Cemetery
Barton rd
A306
Hammersmith br
Wharf
Distillery rd
Distillery rd
Beryl rd
Claxton gro
Comeragh rd
Castle
Winslow rd
St Dunstan's rd
Charing Cross Hospital
Claxton gro
Chelmsford st
Norfolk ter
THE QUEENS CLUB
Wharf
Lochaline st
Palfrey st
Claybrook rd
Margravine rd
St Alban's ter
Greyhound rd
Ramsoch rd
Gastein rd
Greyhound rd
Tasso rd
Riverview gdns
Clavering av
Arundel ter
Colwith rd
Rosedew rd
Aspenlea rd
Davies Walk
Adeney clo
Spencer rd
Kinnoul rd
Misard rd
RIVER THAMES
Skelwith rd
Nella rd
Averill st
Delorme st
Bothwell st
Humbolt rd
Disbrowe rd
Bowfell rd
Larnach st
Wingrave rd
Elfaine rd
A3218
400
Lillie road
Crefeld clo
Bayonne
Ancill
Laundry rd
Brecon rd
Ramsoch rd
Silverton rd
Lillie road
A3
Radnville st
Petley rd
Crabtree la
200
300
Chaldon rd
Aintree Estate
Lillie road
THAMES
Wharf
Adam Wlk
Wheatsheaf la
Niton st
FULHAM RECREATION GROUND
Strode rd
Dawes road
200
Rosa Bank
Holport rd
Lysia st
Bronsart rd
Mantret rd
Hannell rd
Mablethorpe rd
Aintree st
Barn Elms Water Works
Wharf
Meadowbank
Stevenage rd
Queensmill rd
Fulham Cemetery
Rowallan rd
Bronsart rd
Rostslane rd
Sherbrooke rd
Langthorne st
Allestree rd
Kingwood rd
Orbain rd
St Olaf's
Kenyon st
A219
Atalanta st
Bankswa st
Purcell
Wyfold rd
Kilmarsh

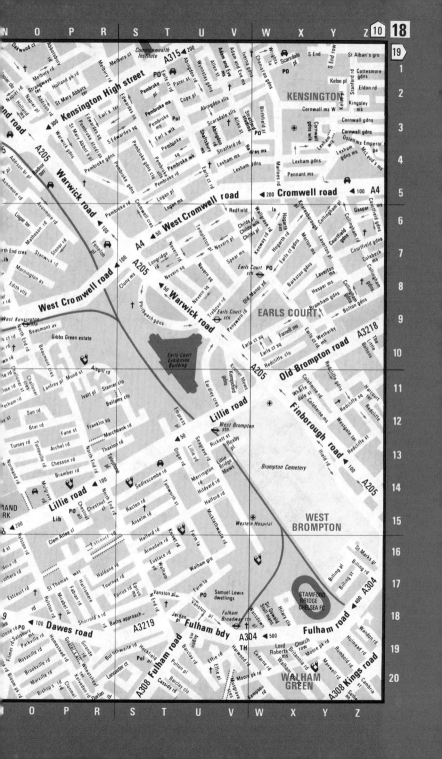

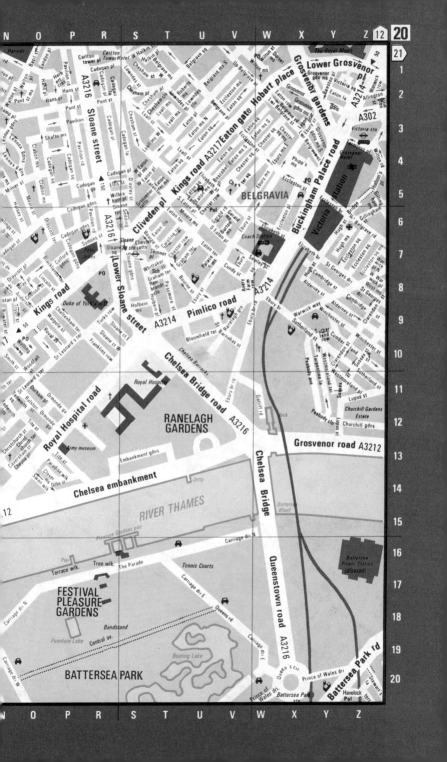

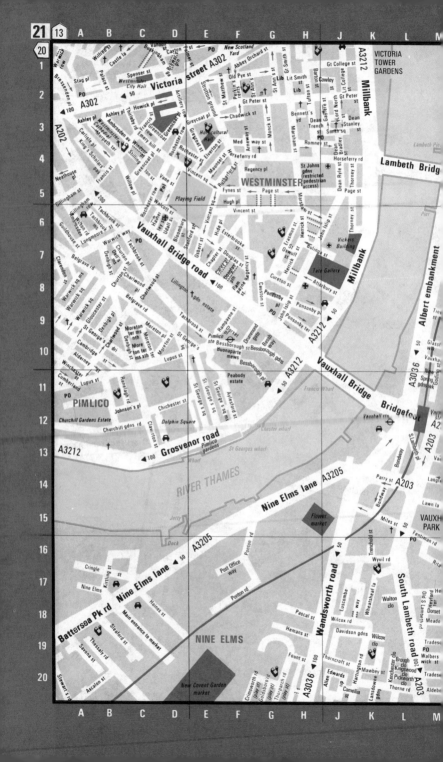

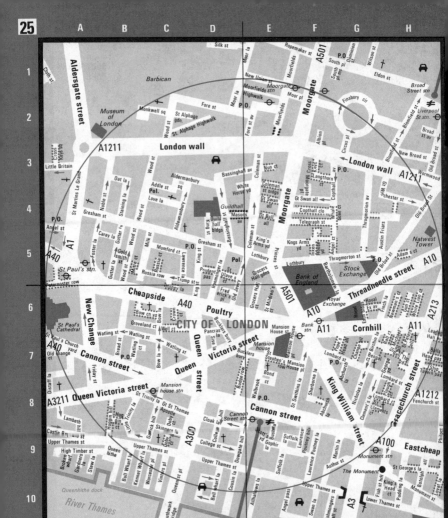

Enlargement of crowded city area for extra clarity

SIGHTSEEING

Tourist information

British Travel Centre **13 E 12**
Rex House, 4–12 Lower Regent St SW1.
Personal callers only. Home of the British
Tourist Authority Information Centre incorporating American Express Travel Service
Office, bureau de change and British Rail
ticket office. Details on where to go throughout the UK. Book a room, coach trip or theatre
ticket; buy plane or train tickets; hire a car; all
under one roof. Also regular exhibitions,
videos, travel book shop and gift shop. *OPEN
09.00–18.30 Mon–Sat, 10.00–16.00 Sun.*
For telephone enquiries 01-730 3400 *Mon–Sat.* No phone bookings.

**London Transport Travel Information
Centres**
London Transport offices for enquiries on
travel (Underground, buses and Green Line
coaches), and general tourist information.
Their booklet *How to get there* is essential.
Also free maps of underground and buses and
tourist maps in French, German, Italian, Spanish and Dutch.
St James's Park Underground Station.
01-222 1234. *24-hr telephone service.*
Oxford Circus Underground Station
Piccadilly Circus Underground Station
ALL OPEN 08.30–21.30 Mon–Sun.

**London Tourist Board
Information Centre** **20 Z 4**
Victoria Station Forecourt SW1. Travel and

tourist information for London and England.
Most languages spoken. Also instant hotel
reservations, theatre and tour bookings, sales
of tourist tickets, guide books and maps.
*OPEN Apr–Nov 08.45–21.30 Mon–Sun;
Nov–Apr 09.00–19.00 Mon–Sat, 09.00–
17.00 Sun.*
Telephone information service: 01-730 3488.
Harrods, Knightsbridge SW1.
Heathrow Central Underground Station
Selfridges, 400 Oxford St W1
Tower of London, West Gate E1

Daily ceremonies

Changing of the Guard **13 A 18**
Buckingham Palace SW1. Takes place inside
the palace railings, in summer the crowd
makes it difficult to see. An alternative is to
see the Guards on their way from Chelsea or
Wellington Barracks; phone the LTB to find
out which they are leaving from on the day
you are going. *Mon–Sun in summer, alternate days in winter.* Leave Chelsea Barracks
at *10.45* or Wellington Barracks at *11.00.*
Palace ceremony *11.30.*

Whitehall SW1 **13 H 15**
Horse Guards Pde SW1. Changing of the
Queen's Life Guard mounted on splendid
black horses. Guards leave Hyde Park Barracks *10.38 Mon–Sat, 09.39 Sun.* Ceremony
11.00 Mon–Sat, 10.00 Sun.

LOOKING AT LONDON

Barbican Centre **15 B 1**
Silk St EC2. Information 01-638 4141 ext 218.
Heralded by jokes about the difficulty of
finding the way into it, the country's largest
arts centre opened in March 1982. A concert
hall, two theatres, three cinemas, a public
library, an art gallery and sculpture court and
two restaurants are among its wealth of facilities. One among many fascinating statistics is
that 130,000 cubic metres of concrete –
enough to build over 19 miles of six-lane
motorway – were used in its construction.

Buckingham Palace **13 A 18**
St James's Park SW1. The permanent London residence of the Sovereign. Originally
built 1705, remodelled by Nash 1825; refaced
1913 by Sir Aston Webb.

Covent Garden Market WC2 **13 L 9**
Originally designed by Inigo Jones as a residential square in the 1630s. Market buildings are of 1830 by Fowler, Floral Hall added in
1860 by E. M. Barry, architect of the Royal

Opera House (1858). In 1974 the market
moved to Nine Elms, but the area survived
threats of redevelopment to become a
flourishing new community, with eclectic,
though expensive, shopping, restaurants and
the London Transport Museum. Street entertainers compete for attention.

Downing St SW1 **13 J 16**
17thC street with houses built by Sir George
Downing. No. 10 is the official residence of
the Prime Minister, No. 11 of the Chancellor
of the Exchequer.

Houses of Parliament **13 K 20**
St Margaret St SW1. 01-219 3000. Victorian-Gothic building 1840–68 by Sir Charles Barry
and A. W. N. Pugin. Westminster Hall was
built in 1099 as the Great Hall of William
Rufus' new palace; the roof dates from the
late 14thC. *Admission to the House of Commons during debates by application to your
MP or by queuing. Tours of Westminster Hall
by application to your MP.*

Kensington Palace   **10 Y 15**
Kensington Gardens W8. 01-937 9561. Unostentatious house bought in 1689 by William III and altered by Wren and William Kent; attribution of the Orangery, of exceptionally fine brick, is uncertain. Queen Victoria and Queen Mary were born here. State apartments and Costume Museum. *OPEN 09.00–17.00 Mon–Sat, 13.00–17.00 Sun. Last tickets sold at 16.30. CLOSED some nat hols. Charge.*

Lambeth Palace   **22 O 3**
Lambeth Palace Rd SE1. 01-928 8282. The London residence of the Archbishop of Canterbury since 1197. Remarkable Tudor gatehouse, fine medieval crypt, 14thC Hall with a splendid roof and portraits of archbishops on its walls. The Great Hall, which houses the library, was rebuilt in medieval style in 1633. *Tours by written application to the Palace Secretary.*

Lloyd's of London   **15 J 7**
Lime St EC3. 01-623 7100. Designed by Richard Rogers & Ptnrs and completed in 1986, this building is the new HQ for the world-famous Lloyd's international insurance market. An impressive and controversial structure gleaming with glass and aluminium, it features the first external glass-sided lifts in Britain. Tours between *10.00–16.00 Mon–Fri.* Book in advance.

Regent's Park Zoo   **4 S 8**
North side of Regent's Park NW1. 01-722 3333. Contains a number of interesting buildings. Gorilla House by Lubetkin & Tecton 1935; Penguin Pool by Tecton 1935; Aviary by Viscount Snowdon, Cedric Price & Frank Newby 1965–6; Elephant House by Casson, Conder & Ptnrs 1965–6; Small Mammal House by Design Research Unit 1967; Sobell Apes & Monkeys Pavilion 1972; and the New Lion Terraces 1970. *OPEN 09.00–18.00 Mon–Sat, 10.00–19.00 Sun & nat hols.*

Royal Albert Hall   **11 E 19**
Kensington Gore SW7. 01-589 8212. Victorian domed hall named after Prince Albert, built 1871. Orchestral, choral, pop concerts, sporting events and public meetings. Famous for the 'Proms'.

Soho W1   **13 E 7**
An area bounded by Regent Street, Oxford Street and Charing Cross Road. Lively and notorious but quite safe, except from touts for peep show, nude encounter and strip joint customers. 18thC streets full of fascinating foreign food shops, restaurants, and night life of all sorts. Visit London's 'Chinatown' around Gerrard Street.

South Bank Arts Centre   **14 O 13**
Waterloo SE1. First came the Royal Festival Hall (Robert Matthew and Leslie Martin, LCC Architect's Department), musical focus of the 1951 Festival of Britain which spurred the redevelopment of this run down area. Most recent is the National Theatre (Denys Lasdun) completed in 1977 with its three auditoria. In between came the Hayward Art Gallery and the Queen Elizabeth Hall and Purcell Room.

St Paul's Cathedral   **14 Z 6**
Ludgate Hill EC4. 01-248 4619/2705. Wren's greatest work; built 1675–1710 replacing the previous church destroyed by the Great Fire. Superb dome, porches and funerary monuments. Contains magnificent stalls by Grinling Gibbons. Ironwork by Tijou, paintings by Thornhill and mosaics by Salviati and Stevens. *OPEN Apr–Sep 08.00–18.00; Oct–Mar 08.00–17.00. Crypt & galleries OPEN 10.00–16.15 Mon–Fri, 11.00–16.15 Sat. To 15.15 winter.*

The Temple   **14 T 8**
Inner Temple, Crown Office Row EC4. 01-353 8462. Middle Temple, Middle Temple Lane EC4. 01-353 4355. Both are Inns of Court. Enter by the gatehouse, 1685, in Middle Temple Lane. An extensive area of courtyards, alleys, gardens and warm brick buildings. Step back into the 19thC on misty winter afternoons when the lamplighter lights the gas lamps. Middle Temple Hall 1570. The restored Temple Church is one of only four remaining early Gothic round churches built by the Templars. 12th–13thC. *Inner Temple OPEN 10.30–11.45 & 15.00–16.00 by arrangement Mon–Fri. CLOSED weekends, nat hols & legal vacations. Middle Temple Hall OPEN 10.00–11.30 & 15.00–16.00 Mon–Fri, 10.00–16.00 Sat. CLOSED Sun, nat hols & during examinations.*

Tower Bridge   **16 N 14**
EC3. 01-407 0922. Victorian-Gothic towers with hydraulic twin drawbridge. Jones and Wolfe Barry 1894. Enter by the tower closest to the Tower of London and take a lift to the high walkways for breathtaking views of London and the Thames. The museum on the other side houses the Victorian steam engines that formerly provided the power to operate the bridge. *OPEN Apr–Oct 10.00–18.30 Mon–Sun; Nov–Mar 10.00–17.30 Mon–Sun. Last admission 45 mins before closing time. Charge.*

Tower of London   **15 M 11**
Tower Hill EC3. 01-709 0765. A keep, a prison and still a fortress. Famous for the Bloody Tower, Traitors' Gate, the ravens, Crown Jewels, the Armouries and the Yeoman Warders. Norman Chapel of St John. *OPEN Mar–Oct 09.30–17.30 Mon–Sat, 14.00–17.00 Sun; Nov–Feb 09.30–16.00 Mon–Sat. Charge.*

Trafalgar Sq WC2   **13 H 12**
Laid out by Sir Charles Barry 1829. Nelson's column (granite) by William Railton 1840. Statue by Baily. Bronze lions by Landseer 1868. Fountains by Lutyens. Famous for political rallies, pigeons and the excesses of New Year's Eve revellers making whoopee.

Westminster Abbey   **13 J 20**
(The Collegiate Church of St Peter in Westminster) Broad Sanctuary SW1. 01-222 5152. Original church by Edward the Confessor 1065. Rebuilding commenced by Henry III in 1245 who was largely influenced by the new French cathedrals. Completed by Henry

Yevele and others 1376–1506 (towers incomplete and finished by Hawksmoor 1734). Henry VII Chapel added 1503; fine perpendicular with wonderful fan vaulting. The Abbey contains the Coronation Chair, and many tombs and memorials of the Kings and Queens of England and their subjects. Starting place for pilgrimage to Canterbury Cathedral. *OPEN 09.00–16.00 Mon–Fri, 09.00–14.00 & 15.45–17.00 Sat. Charge.*

MUSEUMS AND GALLERIES

British Museum **13 H 1**
Great Russell St WC1. 01-636 1555. One of the largest and greatest museums in the world. The Egyptian sculpture gallery on the ground floor was redesigned in 1981 and dramatically highlights colossi of pharaohs, sphinxes, sarcophagi, priests, chantresses, architectural elements and the Rosetta stone. Upstairs mummies preside, striking a chill and thrill to the heart. Cycladic, Bronze Age and Archaic remains are part of an extensive Greek and Roman collection. The Elgin marbles, sculptures from the Parthenon in Athens, are characterised by fluidity of line and generate a sense of occasion and excitement. Be sure to see the colossal winged lion and bull with human heads in the Assyrian Transept, the sculptures from the throne-room of the palace at Nimrud, the sculpture of the transport of a colossal winged bull in the Nineveh Gallery, harps and lyres in the Babylonian Room. Building 1823–47 by Sir Robert Smirke; the domed reading room 1857 is by Sidney Smirke. *OPEN 10.00–17.00 Mon–Sat, 14.30–18.00 Sun. Films Tue–Fri, lectures Tue–Sat, gallery talks. Free.*

Museum of London **15 A 2**
London Wall EC2. 01-600 3699. Combined collections of the former London Museum and Guildhall Museum with extra material. A 3-dimensional history of the City and London area, with models, reconstructions and even the Lord Mayor's Coach. *OPEN 10.00–18.00 Tue–Sat, 14.00–18.00 Sun. Closed Mon & nat hols. Free.*

National Gallery **13 H 11**
Trafalgar Sq WC2. 01-839 3321. Very fine representative collection of various schools of painting. Includes many world famous pictures. Rich in early Italian (Leonardo da Vinci, Raphael, Botticelli and Titian), Dutch and Flemish (Rembrandt, Rubens, Frans Hals, Van Dyck), Spanish 15–18thC (Velasquez and El Greco), British 18th and 19thC (Constable, Turner, Gainsborough and Reynolds). An information sheet, *A Quick Visit to the National Gallery*, leads the time-pressed to 16 masterpieces. Daily guided tours highlight selected pictures. Building 1838 by W. Wilkins. *OPEN 10.00–18.00 Mon–Sat, 14.00–18.00 Sun. Free.*

National Portrait Gallery **13 H 11**
2 St Martin's Pl WC2. 01-930 1552. Historic collection of contemporary portraits of famous British men and women, forming a fascinating study of human personality. Start with the Tudors on the top floor, portrayed with varying degrees of vivacity and truthfulness. Note the contrast between the Sittow portrait of Henry VII as shrewd statesman and his representation by Holbein as saintly sage. Shakespeare looks strangely modern with an earring in his left ear.
The Victorians dominate the first floor, arranged according to whether their designs were philanthropic, political, colonial or artistic. The haggard faces of Thomas Carlyle, John Stuart Mill and Matthew Arnold seem better to reflect the struggle with doubt engendered by Charles Darwin's theory of evolution and the ascendency of the machine, than the smooth young faces of Dickens and Tennyson among the early Victorians.
There are even more striking contrasts among the Edwardians, such as the ruthless resolve of Kitchener, softness and sensitivity of Lawrence of Arabia, brilliance and effeteness visible in Aubrey Beardsley's portraits and the rotund avuncular presences of Gilbert and Sullivan. On the ground floor is the 20thC gallery with exciting revolving displays arranged by theme. Prince Charles and Princess Diana feature here. Excellent reference section of engravings and photographs. *OPEN 10.00–17.00 Mon–Fri, 10.00–18.00 Sat, 14.00–18.00 Sun. CLOSED nat hols. Free.*

Natural History Museum **19 F 4**
Cromwell Rd SW7. 01-589 6323. The national collections of zoology, entomology, palaeontology, mineralogy and botany. Built in Romanesque style by A. Waterhouse, 1879, and decorated with terracotta mouldings of animals and plants. Dinosaurs are among the favourite exhibits. They tower in the central hall and the apses to the left are devoted to their evolution, lifestyle and extinction. Computer games can be played to see which animals share which characteristics, such as four bony limbs or a back-bone. Visit the Hall of Human Biology and find out how your nervous system, brain and muscles function. Upstairs man meets his animal relatives and his closeness to chimpanzees and gorillas is examined. Darwin's theory of the origin of species is explored with many audio-visual aids and computers to help you get things straight. The 90ft model blue whale is a staggering sight among the marine mammals.

OPEN 10.00–18.00 Mon–Sat, 14.30–18.00 Sun. Charge.

Science Museum 19 G 2
Exhibition Rd SW7. 01-589 3456. The history of science and its application to industry. A large collection of very fine engineering models, steam engines, early motor cars, aeroplanes and all aspects of applied physics and chemistry. Explore the history of printing, textiles, and many other industries through working models. Special features include exploration under the sea and into outer space, with the actual Apollo 10 space capsule and life-size reconstruction of the Apollo 11 lunar lander. The Wellcome galleries examine the history of medicine with thoroughness. *OPEN 10.00–18.00 Mon–Sat, 14.30–18.00 Sun. CLOSED nat hols. Free lectures & films, or write for brochure. Free.*

Tate Gallery 21 J 7
Millbank SW1. 01-821 1313. Representative collections of British painting from the 16thC to the present day; fine examples of Blake, Hogarth, the pre-Raphaelites, Ben Nicolson, Spenser and Francis Bacon; sculpture by Moore, Hepworth. Also a particularly rich collection of foreign paintings and sculpture from 1880 to the present day, including paintings by Picasso, Chagall, Mondrian, Pollock, Lichtenstein, Rothko, Degas, Marini and Giacometti. Designed 1897 by Sidney H. J. Smith. The Clore Gallery opened in spring 1987 to house the Turner Bequest. *OPEN 10.00–18.00 Mon–Sat, 14.00–18.00 Sun. Lectures at various times. Free.*

Victoria and Albert Museum 19 H 3
Cromwell Rd SW7. 01-589 6371. A museum of decorative art, comprising vast European and Far Eastern collections from all ages. Over 10 acres of museum. Three former refreshment rooms by William Morris, James Gamble and Sir Edward Poynter, were saved from demolition, and the exuberant decoration of ceramic, stained glass, enamel, tiles, and panels painted by Burne-Jones, renovated; the Victorian plastercast courts have been refurbished to match their pristine 1873 condition, and Trajan's column, cast in Rome in 1864, is among the exhibits.
Fine Art collections include Sandby, Girtin, Cotman, Constable, Turner and cartoons by Raphael. The Prints and Drawings Dept has extensive collections dealing with art, architecture, pure and applied design and graphics. In the furniture collection is the 16thC Great Bed of Ware. Sculpture, ecclesiastical art, carpets, tapestries, metalwork and Indian and Far Eastern art are all comprehensively represented. *OPEN 10.00–17.50 Mon–Thur & Sat, 14.30–17.50 Sun. CLOSED Fri. Free lectures at various times. Voluntary admission charge.*

PARKS AND GARDENS

Hyde Park W1 12 O 13
01-262 5484. A Royal Park since 1536, it was once part of the forest reserved by Henry VIII for hunting wild boar and bulls. Queen Elizabeth I held military reviews here (still held on special occasions). It was the haunt of highwaymen until 1750 and even today is patrolled at night by police. The Great Exhibition of 1851 designed by Paxton was held opposite Prince of Wales Gate. Hyde Park now has 340 acres of parkland. Rotten Row for horse-riders, and the Serpentine – a fine natural lake for boating and swimming. The Serpentine Bridge is by George Rennie 1826. The famous 'Speaker's Corner' is near Marble Arch – public executions were held at Tyburn gallows nearby until 1783. Good open-air bar and restaurant overlooking the lake (near the bridge). *OPEN 05.00–24.00. No cars after dusk. The Lido OPEN May–Sep & hols 10.00 –20.00 for swimming. Charge for swimming.*

Kensington Gardens W8 11 D 13
01-937 4848. A formal and elegant addition to Hyde Park. 275 acres of Royal Park containing William III's lovely Kensington Palace, Queen Anne's Orangery, the peaceful 'Sunken Garden' nearby, the Round Pond with its busy model sailing-boats and, to the south, the magnificently Victorian 'Albert Memorial'. The famous Broad Walk, until recently flanked by ancient elms is now replanted with fragrant limes and maples and the nearby 'Flower Walk' is the home of wild birds, woodpeckers, flycatchers and tree-creepers. Queen Caroline created both the Long Water (Peter Pan's statue is here) and the Serpentine by damming the Westbourne river. Good children's playground. *Open 07.30–dusk.*

Green Park 12 Y 16
SW1. 01-930 1793. Its 53 acres were enclosed by Henry VIII and made into a Royal Park by Charles II who had the walks laid out. Popular during the 18thC as a venue for duels, balloon ascents and as a haunt for highwaymen, it is now a quiet green space to sit in a deckchair under the trees. *OPEN 05.00– 24.00.*

St James's Park 13 E 17
SW1. 01-930 1793. The oldest Royal Park, acquired in 1532 by Henry VIII, laid out in imitation 'Versailles' style by Charles II, finally redesigned in the grand manner for George IV by John Nash in the 1820s. The bird sanctuary on Duck Island has pelicans and over 20 species of duck and goose. Good views of Buckingham Palace, the domes and spires of Whitehall and to the south, Westminster Abbey. *OPEN 05.00–24.00.*

A

3	C 9	Abbey gdns NW8
21	F 1	Abbey Orchard st SW1
2	Y 4	Abbey rd NW6
3	B 7	Abbey rd NW8
16	O 20	Abbey st SE1
24	Z 5	Abbeyfield rd SE16
15	K 14	Abbots la SE1
2	W 3	Abbots pl NW6
0	N 19	Abbotsbury clo W14
10	N 19	Abbotsbury rd W14
9	A 14	Abdale rd W12
3	C 11	Abercorn clo NW8
3	C 10	Abercorn pl NW8
2	Z 1	Aberdare gdns NW6
3	A 1	Aberdare gdns NW6
3	F 17	Aberdeen pl NW8
23	J 4	Aberdour st SE1
18	U 1	Abingdon rd W8
21	K 2	Abingdon st SW1
18	U 2	Abingdon vlls W8
2	S 16	Abinger ms W9
24	Z 10	Ablett st SE16
2	G 8	Acacia gdns NW8
3	G 8	Acacia pl NW8
3	G 8	Acacia rd NW8
10	O 1	Acklam rd W10
2	W 1	Acol rd NW6
7	M 3	Acton ms E8
6	O 13	Acton st WC1
8	V 7	Ada pl E2
23	H 20	Ada rd SE5
8	V 5	Ada st E8
1	M 18	Adair rd W10
13	B 4	Adam & Eve ct W1
18	V 1	Adam & Eve ms W8
13	L 10	Adam St WC2
12	V 10	Adams row W1
17	E 18	Adams wlk SW6
23	D 16	Addington sq SE5
14	P 18	Addington st SE1
9	K 15	Addison av W11
18	N 4	Addison Br pl W14
9	M 20	Addison cres W14
17	M 1	Addison cres W14
9	G 20	Addison gdns W14
17	F 1	Addison gdns W14
3	J 15	Addison rd W14
18	O 2	Addison rd W14
9	M 18	Addison rd W14
14	Y 7	Addle hill EC4
1	K 17	Adela st W10
3	H 1	Adelaide rd NW3
13	J 11	Adelaide st WC2
Z	20	Adelina gro E1
13	G 3	Adeline pl WC1
13	L 11	Adelphi ter WC2
17	H 15	Adeney clo W6
17	U 16	Adeney rd W6
17	A 3	Adie rd W6
16	S 4	Adler st E1
1	H 18	Admiral ms W10
3	G 20	Adpar st W2
0	O 10	Affleck st N1
5	D 1	Agar gro NW1
13	K 10	Agar st WC2
17	A 3	Agate rd W6
16	Y 12	Agatha clo E1
6	W 15	Agdon st EC1
4	P 2	Ainger ms NW8
4	P 2	Ainger rd NW3
8	X 14	Ainsley st E2
3	A 4	Ainsworth way NW8
17	L 18	Aintree st SW6
13	D 10	Air st W1
6	N 2	Airdrie clo N1
10	S 15	Airlie gdns W8
8	R 5	Aitken clo E8
14	T 16	Alaska st SE1
10	N 4	Alba pl W11
13	B 11	Albany ctyd W1

23	M 10	Albany rd SE1
23	C 15	Albany rd SE17
23	H 13	Albany rd SE5
4	X 8	Albany st NW1
13	A 12	Albemarle st W1
6	W 18	Albemarle way EC1
19	M 18	Albert Br rd SW11
20	N 20	Albert Br rd SW11
19	M 16	Albert br SW11
14	N 17	Albert emb SE1
21	M 18	Albert emb SE1
12	R 17	Albert ga SW1
12	R 17	Albert ga SW1
11	F 19	Albert Hall mans SW7
19	A 1	Albert ms W8
10	Z 20	Albert pl W8
2	R 9	Albert rd NW6
22	N 20	Albert sq SW8
4	Z 8	Albert st NW1
4	S 4	Albert Ter ms NW1
4	S 5	Albert ter NW1
22	X 9	Alberta st SE17
11	L 8	Albion clo W2
8	O 2	Albion dri E8
6	T 2	Albion ms N1
11	L 7	StAlbion ms W2
6	I 9	Albion pl EC1
8	O 1	Albion sq E8
11	L 8	Albion st W2
8	N 1	Albion ter E8
23	J 9	Aldbridge st SE17
21	M 20	Aldebert ter SW8
22	N 20	Aldebert ter SW8
5	D 10	Aldenham sr SW1
24	O 16	Alder clo SE15
9	F 6	Aldermans st W10
15	J 3	Aldermans wlk EC2
24	S 9	Alderminster rd SE1
21	A 10	Alderney st SW1
20	X 8	Alderney st SW1
15	A 1	Aldersgate st EC1
2	R 3	Aldershot rd NW6
1	L 16	Alderson st W10
12	T 12	Aldford st W1
15	M 6	Aldgate EC3
16	O 5	Aldgate High st E1
9	E 16	Aldine st W12
10	R 3	Aldridge Rd Vlls W11
2	X 19	Aldsworth clo W9
14	O 7	Aldwych WC2
1	A 2	Alexander av NW10
10	W 4	Alexander ms W2
19	J 4	Alexander pl SW7
19	J 4	Alexander sq SW7
10	W 4	Alexander st W2
3	C 3	Alexandra clo NW8
3	C 3	Alexandra pl NW8
3	D 3	Alexandra rd NW8
24	T 5	Alexis st SE16
5	E 20	Alfred ms W1
13	E 1	Alfred pl W1
10	U 1	Alfred rd W2
2	S 5	Algernon rd NW6
23	J 2	Alice st SE1
16	R 6	Alie st E1
5	M 7	All Saints rd N1
10	O 3	All Saints rd W11
6	N 7	All Saints st N1
1	A 4	All Souls av NW10
12	Z 2	All Souls pl W1
21	J 20	Allen Edwards dri SW8
18	U 1	Allen st W8
17	K 19	Allestree rd SW6
6	Z 7	Alliance st N1
7	A 7	Allingham st N1
1	K 10	Allington rd W10
20	Z 2	Allington st SW1
3	K 8	Allitsen rd NW8
4	R 18	Allsop pl NW1
24	P 6	Alma gro SE1

3	D 11	Alma Sq NW8
6	W 3	Almeida st N1
24	X 6	Almond rd SE16
7	F 1	Almorah st N1
2	N 16	Alperton st W10
3	L 15	Alpha clo NW1
2	U 8	Alpha pl NW8
19	M 13	Alpha pl SW3
23	H 10	Alsace rd SE17
24	O 5	Alscot rd SE1
23	J 9	Alvey st SE17
16	V 6	Amazon st E1
13	B 16	Ambassadors ct SW1
22	X 10	Ambergate st SE17
2	W 19	Amberley rd W9
21	B 3	Ambrosden av SW1
24	V 6	Ambrose st SE16
23	A 8	Amelia st SE17
22	Z 8	Amelia st SE17
14	Y 5	Amen corner EC4
14	Y 5	Amen ct EC4
16	N 8	America sq EC3
15	A 15	America st SE1
1	A 5	Amery gdns NW10
17	A 2	Amor rd W6
6	N 13	Ampton pl WC1
6	N 14	Ampton st WC1
6	S 12	Amwell st EC1
24	W 6	Anchor st SE16
17	J 15	Ancill clo W6
20	N 8	Anderson st SW3
2	X 9	Andover pl NW6
8	X 6	Andrews rd E8
16	P 3	Angel all E1
13	C 14	Angel ct SW1
6	T 9	Angel ms N1
14	Z 4	Angel st EC1
15	A 4	Angel st EC1
17	B 8	Angel wlk W6
8	U 18	Anglesea st E1
19	L 19	Anhalt rd SW11
9	E 20	Anley rd W14
19	F 16	Ann la SW10
8	R 4	Anna clo E8
12	S 19	Anns clo SW1
16	O 2	Anns pl E1
10	Y 20	Ansdell st W8
10	Y 20	Ansdell ter W8
18	S 15	Anselm rd SW6
9	H 10	Ansleigh pl W11
19	F 17	Apollo pl SW10
14	W 7	Apothecary st EC4
13	D 12	Apple Tree yd SW1
8	N 8	Appleby st E2
1	M 18	Appleford rd W10
17	G 3	Applegarth rd W14
7	J 20	Appold st EC2
3	H 8	Aquila st NW8
14	T 14	Aquinas st SE1
7	M 2	Arbutus st E8
15	J 2	Arcade the EC2
23	A 3	Arch st SE1
22	O 2	Archbishops park SE11
18	P 13	Archel rd W14
13	E 9	Archer st W1
11	M 7	Archery clo W2
12	W 11	Archibald ms W1
14	Z 16	Argent st SE1
18	U 19	Argon ms SW6
5	L 12	Argyle sq WC1
5	L 13	Argyle st WC1
10	U 20	Argyll rd W8
13	A 6	Argyll st W1
9	D 12	Ariel way W12
7	D 6	Arlington av N1
5	A 8	Arlington rd NW1
4	Y 5	Arlington rd NW1
7	C 6	Arlington sq N1
13	A 13	Arlington st SW1
6	U 12	Arlington way EC1
18	T 16	Armadale rd SW6
13	L 6	Arne st SW2

21 F 3	Arneway st SW1	
8 N 14	Arnold cir E2	
23 D 13	Arnside st SE17	
10 T 6	Artesian rd W2	
16 V 10	Artichoke hill E1	
15 L 1	Artillery la E1	
15 M 2	Artillery pas E1	
21 D 2	Artillery row SW1	
10 N 8	Arundel gdns W11	
14 P 8	Arundel st WC2	
17 A 14	Arundel ter SW13	
21 B 20	Ascalon st SW8	
8 X 5	Ash gro E8	
3 K 18	Ashbridge rd NW8	
19 A 5	Ashburn gdns SW7	
19 A 5	Ashburn pl SW7	
1 C 11	Ashburnham rd NW10	
19 D 19	Ashburnham rd SW10	
6 X 13	Ashby st EC1	
17 A 7	Ashcroft sq W6	
16 W 3	Ashfield st E1	
12 T 1	Ashland pl W1	
21 B 3	Ashley pl SW1	
3 L 19	Ashmill st NW1	
22 O 15	Ashmole estate SW8	
22 R 16	Ashmole pl SW8	
22 R 16	Ashmole st SW8	
2 O 11	Ashmore rd W9	
2 Y 13	Ashworth rd W9	
17 G 14	Aspenlea rd W6	
24 Y 5	Aspinden rd SE16	
15 S 4	Assam st E1	
19 L 9	Astell st SW3	
6 Z 1	Astleys row N1	
9 B 20	Astrop ms W6	
9 B 20	Astrop ter W6	
19 A 6	Astwood ms SW5	
24 X 16	Asylum rd SE15	
19 C 4	Atherstone ms SW7	
17 J 20	Atlanta st SW6	
21 H 8	Atterbury st SW1	
6 S 15	Attneave st WC1	
3 B 10	Aubrey pl NW8	
10 P 14	Aubrey rd W8	
10 R 15	Aubrey wlk W8	
22 N 11	Auckland st SE11	
4 T 3	Auden pl NW1	
12 V 13	Audley sq W1	
8 T 8	Audrey st E2	
17 F 3	Augustine rd W14	
4 Z 11	Augustus st NW1	
22 U 12	Aulton pl SE11	
17 K 6	Auriol rd W14	
7 M 14	Austin st E2	
22 W 4	Austral st SE11	
14 Y 6	Ave Maria la EC4	
7 F 5	Avebury st N1	
22 R 10	Aveline st SE11	
3 L 6	Avenue clo NW8	
3 J 4	Avenue rd NW8	
1 J 4	Avenue the NW6	
17 G 15	Averill st W6	
20 V 8	Avery Farm row SW1	
12 X 8	Avery row W1	
9 K 11	Avondale park W11	
9 J 10	Avondale Pk gdns W11	
9 J 9	Avondale Pk rd W11	
24 S 11	Avondale sq SE1	
18 N 4	Avonmore rd W14	
18 N 5	Avonmore rd W14	
23 A 1	Avonmouth st SE1	
12 T 2	Aybrook st W1	
6 W 17	Aylesbury st EC1	
21 F 11	Aylesford st SW1	
1 F 2	Aylestone av NW6	
17 H 3	Aynhoe rd W14	
15 B 16	Ayres st SE1	

B

13 E 12	Babmaes st SW1	
7 G 13	Baches st N1	

16 T 5	Back Ch la E1	
6 T 18	Back hill EC1	
23 M 3	Bacon gro SE1	
8 R 16	Bacon st E2	
15 F 17	Baden Pl SE1	
23 B 20	Badsworth rd SE5	
23 K 10	Bagshot st SE17	
13 G 4	Bainbridge st WC1	
4 R 19	Baker st NW1	
12 S 2	Baker st W1	
15 K 14	Bakers all SE1	
12 T 4	Bakers ms W1	
6 T 17	Bakers row EC1	
24 P 6	Balaclava rd SE1	
4 N 18	Balcombe st NW1	
12 U 7	Balderton st W1	
7 E 14	Baldwin st EC1	
7 A 8	Baldwin ter N1	
6 S 20	Baldwins gdns EC1	
5 L 9	Balfe st N1	
12 U 12	Balfour ms W1	
12 U 11	Balfour pl W1	
23 D 5	Balfour st SE17	
9 E 5	Balliol rd W10	
7 G 3	Balmes rd N1	
7 A 18	Baltic st EC1	
9 D 18	Bamborough gdns W12	
13 K 8	Banbury ct WC2	
1 G 12	Banister rd NW10	
15 D 12	Bank end SE1	
15 A 11	Bankside SE1	
7 B 18	Banner st EC1	
23 F 19	Bantry st SE5	
24 X 3	Banyard rd SE16	
17 D 3	Barb ms W6	
22 V 1	Barbel st SE1	
18 T 20	Barclay clo SW6	
18 U 19	Barclay rd SW6	
9 G 10	Bard rd W10	
2 N 15	Barfett st W10	
9 F 7	Barfield way W10	
6 U 6	Barford st N1	
14 U 11	Barge Ho st SE1	
7 E 5	Baring st N1	
19 B 14	Barker st SW10	
24 W 11	Barkin way SE16	
24 W 11	Barkis way SE16	
18 X 7	Barkston gdns SW5	
1 G 18	Barlby gdns W10	
1 F 19	Barlby rd W10	
14 Y 2	Barley Mow pass EC1	
12 Z 10	Barlow pl W1	
23 G 6	Barlow st SE17	
17 A 19	Barn Elms Water Works SW13	
14 T 3	Barnards Inn EC4	
5 C 11	Barnby st NW1	
8 S 13	Barnet gro E2	
15 K 16	Barnham st SE1	
6 S 5	Barnsbury rd N1	
6 S 1	Barnsbury sq N1	
6 V 1	Barnsbury st N1	
6 R 1	Barnsbury ter N1	
2 R 16	Barnsdale rd W9	
8 X 17	Barnsley st E1	
6 Z 4	Barnston wlk	
2 Y 19	Barnwood clo W9	
6 T 9	Baron st N1	
8 O 12	Baroness rd E2	
18 N 10	Barons Ct rd W14	
17 L 10	Barons Ct rd W14	
17 K 8	Barons keep W14	
14 V 18	Barons pl SE1	
12 U 6	Barrett st W1	
5 M 20	Barron clo WC1	
3 J 10	Barrow Hill rd NW8	
13 L 3	Barter st WC1	
14 Z 2	Bartholomew clo EC1	
15 A 2	Bartholomew pl EC1	
7 C 15	Bartholomew sq EC1	

23 F 3	Bartholomew st SE1	
9 J 6	Bartle rd W11	
14 U 4	Bartlett ct EC4	
17 L 10	Barton rd W14	
21 H 2	Barton st SW1	
12 O 19	Basil st SW3	
7 L 12	Basing pl E2	
10 O 4	Basing st W11	
7 C 3	Basire st N1	
9 J 3	Bassett rd W10	
6 Z 16	Bastwick st EC1	
7 A 16	Bastwick st EC1	
6 T 6	Batchelor st N1	
13 F 6	Bateman st W1	
13 F 6	Batemans bldgs W1	
7 L 15	Batemans row EC2	
7 J 14	Bath pl EC2	
7 D 14	Bath st EC1	
23 A 2	Bath ter SE1	
1 A 10	Bathurst gdns NW10	
11 G 8	Bathurst ms W2	
11 G 8	Bathurst st W2	
17 D 1	Batoum gdns W6	
19 J 19	Battersea Br rd SW11	
19 H 18	Battersea Br SW11	
19 J 20	Battersea Ch rd SW11	
21 A 18	Battersea Pk rd SW8	
20 Z 20	Battersea Pk rd SW11	
20 R 20	Battersea pk SW11	
6 W 2	Battishill st N1	
15 J 14	Battle Bridge la SE1	
5 J 9	Battle Bridge rd NW1	
16 T 5	Batty st E1	
8 S 11	Baxendale st E2	
17 J 14	Bayarne rd development W6	
1 E 13	Bayford rd NW10	
8 X 2	Bayford st E8	
5 B 7	Bayham pl NW1	
5 A 4	Bayham st NW1	
4 Z 3	Bayham st NW1	
5 B 7	Bayham st NW1	
13 F 2	Bayley st WC1	
14 T 19	Baylis rd SE1	
5 C 2	Baynes st NW1	
17 K 16	Bayonne rd W6	
11 K 9	Bayswater rd W2	
10 W 11	Bayswater rd W2	
11 A 11	Bayswater rd W2	
17 K 3	Beaconsfield Ter rd W14	
17 C 6	Beadon rd W6	
13 B 8	Beak st W1	
13 C 8	Beak st W1	
14 W 4	Bear all EC4	
19 M 2	Beauchamp pl SW3	
19 M 1	Beaufort gdns SW3	
13 G 2	Bedford av WC1	
24 V 10	Bedwin way SE16	
7 A 20	Beech st EC1	
20 Y 2	Beeston pl SW1	
1 L 11	Beethoven st W10	
2 Z 7	Belgrave gdns NW8	
3 A 6	Belgrave gdns NW8	
12 S 20	Belgrave ms north SW1	
20 U 1	Belgrave ms S SW1	
20 T 1	Belgrave ms W SW1	
20 U 3	Belgrave pl SW1	
20 Z 6	Belgrave rd SW1	
21 C 8	Belgrave rd SW1	
12 T 20	Belgrave sq SW1	
20 U 1	Belgrave sq SW1	
20 W 2	Belgrave yd SW1	
5 K 12	Belgrove st WC1	
15 M 2	Bell la E1	
16 N 3	Bell la E1	
3 K 20	Bell st NW1	
11 J 1	Bell st NW1	

14 S 6   Bell yd WC2
18 R 11   Bellamy clo SW5
3 D 1   Belsize rd NW6
2 Z 3   Belsize rd NW6
3 C 2   Belsize rd NW6
14 Z 19   Belvedere bldgs SE1
14 Z 19   Belvedere pl SE1
14 O 18   Belvedere rd SE1
5 M 3   Bemerton st N1
24 U 1   Ben Smith way SE16
17 A 1   Benbow rd W6
3 M 20   Bendall ms NW1
23 G 20   Benhill rd SE5
8 V 4   Benjamin clo E8
6 W 20   Benjamin st EC1
13 A 13   Bennet st SW1
21 H 3   Bennetts yd SW1
12 V 3   Bentinck ms W1
12 V 4   Bentinck st W1
9 A 6   Bentworth rd W12
7 G 3   Benyon rd N1
1 F 13   Berens rd NW10
10 V 14   Berkeley gdns W8
12 R 5   Berkeley ms W1
12 Y 11   Berkeley sq W1
12 Z 12   Berkeley st W1
4 S 1   Berkley gro NW1
4 R 1   Berkley rd NE1
23 K 1   Bermondsey sq SE1
15 J 17   Bermondsey st SE1
16 R 16   Bermondsey Wall
     west SE16
16 U 18   Bermondsey Wall
     east SE16
5 K 18   Bernard st WC1
13 C 2   Berners ms W1
13 D 4   Berners pl W1
6 V 6   Berners rd N1
13 C 3   Berners st W1
6 X 14   Berry pl EC1
6 X 16   Berry st EC1
22 Y 10   Berryfield rd SE17
13 C 5   Berwick st W1
17 F 11   Beryl rd W6
21 F 10   Bessborough pl SW1
21 F 10   Bessborough st SW1
8 U 14   Bethnal Green rd
     E2
8 Z 11   Bethnel Green
     musuem E2
23 C 17   Bethwin rd SE5
22 Z 17   Bethwin rd SE5
13 K 5   Betterton st WC2
7 B 6   Bevan st N1
7 G 12   Bevenden st N1
6 R 11   Bevin way WC1
10 N 2   Bevington rd W10
9 M 1   Bevington rd W10
16 U 18   Bevington st SE16
15 L 4   Bevis marks EC3
16 Z B   Bewley st E1
24 R 14   Bianca rd SE15
4 P 20   Bickenhall st W1
5 H 13   Bidborough st WC1
2 Y 14   Biddulph rd W9
18 Y 17   Billing pl SW10
18 Z 16   Billing rd SW10
18 Y 17   Billing st SW10
15 K 7   Billiter st EC3
19 B 8   Bina gdns SW5
5 M 3   Bingfield st N1
6 N 3   Bingfield st N1
4 T 19   Bingham pl W1
12 V 8   Binney st W1
2 V 4   Birchington rd NW6
12 V 6   Bird st W1
24 R 17   Bird-in-Bush rd
     SE15
13 C 19   Birdcage wlk SW1
23 J 15   Birdlip clo SE15
8 Y 14   Birkbeck st E2
17 F 11   Biscay rd W6
17 L 5   Bishop Kings rd W14

7 B 4   Bishop st N1
11 B 4   Bishops Bridge rd
     W2
14 X 4   Bishops ct EC4
14 R 4   Bishops ct WC2
18 O 20   Bishops rd SW6
22 T 5   Bishops ter SE11
8 Y 8   Bishops way E2
15 J 3   Bishopsgate chyd
     EC2
15 K 3   Bishopsgatge EC2
15 A 18   Bittern st SE1
8 N 19   Black Eagle st E1
23 F 1   Black Horse ct SE1
16 S 2   Black Lion yd E1
22 O 7   Black Prince rd
     SE11
15 K 17   Black Swan yd
     SE1
7 H 16   Blackall st EC2
12 T 10   Blackburnes ms W1
14 V 9   Blackfriars
     underpass EC4
14 W 10   Blackfriars br EC4
14 X 8   Blackfriars la EC4
14 W 17   Blackfriars rd SE1
20 O 7   Blacklands ter SW3
17 B 8   Blacks rd W6
7 L 2   Blackshaw pl N1
23 D 10   Blackwood st SE17
10 N 2   Blagrove rd W10
23 L 19   Blakes rd SE15
24 Z 19   Blanch clo SE15
3 M 18   Blandford sq NW1
12 T 3   Blandford st W1
19 E 18   Blantyre st SW10
14 U 1   Bleeding Heart
     yd EC1
9 L 7   Blenheim cres W11
10 N 6   Blenheim cres W11
3 B 8   Blenheim pas NW8
3 C 7   Blenheim rd NW8
12 X 7   Blenheim st W1
3 B 8   Blenheim ter NW8
7 C 10   Bletchley st N1
18 W 3   Blithfield st W8
3 E 18   Blomfield rd W9
2 Z 20   Blomfield rd W9
15 H 3   Blomfield st EC2
10 Z 1   Blomfield vlls W2
18 N 20   Bloom Pk rd SW6
21 D 6   Bloomburg st SW1
12 Y 8   Bloomfield pl W1
20 U 9   Bloomfield ter SW1
13 L 3   Bloomsbury clo WC1
13 L 1   Bloomsbury pl WC1
13 K 1   Bloomsbury sq WC1
13 H 2   Bloomsbury st WC1
13 K 3   Bloomsbury way WC1
7 M 19   Blossom st E1
23 B 20   Blucher rd SE5
24 V 5   Blue Anchor la
     SE16
13 B 14   Blue Bell yd SW1
17 K 3   Blythe rd W14
17 F 1   Blythe rd W14
8 V 12   Blythe st E2
6 N 6   Boadicea st N1
24 P 18   Boathouse wlk SE15
8 X 4   Bocking st E8
9 H 20   Bolingbroke rd W14
17 G 1   Bolingbroke rd W14
22 N 18   Bolney st SW8
4 Z 20   Bolsover st W1
14 U 6   Bolt ct EC4
22 V 17   Bolton cres SE5
19 A 10   Bolton gdns ms SW5
1 F 10   Bolton gdns NW10
19 A 8   Bolton gdns SW5
2 Z 6   Bolton rd NW8
12 Z 13   Bolton st W1
19 B 10   Boltons the SW10
24 V 5   Bombay st SE16

9 J 8   Bomore rd W11
24 R 20   Bonar rd SE15
9 K 1   Bonchurch rd W10
21 K 14   Bondway SW8
7 G 18   Bonhill st EC2
22 N 14   Bonnington sq SW8
5 A 1   Bonny st NW1
23 J 18   Bonsor st SE5
7 H 14   Boot st N1
13 B 3   Booths pl W1
15 B 19   Borough High st
     SE1
14 Y 20   Borough rd SE1
15 A 19   Borough rd SE1
22 Z 10   Borrett rd SE17
20 V 4   Boscobel pl SW1
3 G 19   Boscobel st NW8
16 N 16   Boss st SE1
4 N 18   Boston pl NW1
8 S 9   Boston st E2
5 M 20   Boswell ct WC1
5 M 20   Boswell st WC1
1 L 18   Bosworth rd W10
17 G 15   Bothwell st W6
10 V 6   Botts ms W2
10 U 6   Botts pass W2
23 C 14   Boundary la SE17
3 C 4   Boundary ms NW8
3 D 4   Boundary rd NW8
14 W 17   Boundary row SE1
13 E 7   Bourchier st W1
12 X 9   Bourdon pl W1
12 Y 9   Bourdon st W1
13 B 2   Bourlet clo W1
20 S 7   Bourne st SW1
10 X 1   Bourne ter W2
14 U 7   Bouverie st EC4
11 H 4   Boverie pl W2
13 L 7   Bow st WC2
22 T 10   Bowden st SE11
17 E 15   Bowfell rd W6
24 S 13   Bowles rd SE1
15 E 17   Bowling Green pl
     SE1
22 T 13   Bowling Green st
     SE11
7 H 12   Bowling Green wlk
     N1
6 U 17   Bowling grn la EC1
23 D 18   Bowyer pl SE5
23 B 18   Bowyer st SE5
6 R 4   Boxworth gr N1
16 T 7   Boyd st E1
3 F 2   Boydell ct NW8
14 Y 19   Boyfield st SE1
13 A 9   Boyle st W1
10 O 13   Boyne Ter ms W11
23 D 14   Boyston rd SE17
24 X 11   Boythorn way SE16
9 A 2   Bracewell rd W10
7 B 19   Brackley st EC1
14 U 15   Brad st SE1
2 X 18   Braden st W9
2 R 12   Bradiston rd W9
6 T 9   Bradleys clo N1
8 X 20   Brady st E1
22 W 10   Braganza st SE17
16 P 5   Braham st E1
15 K 14   Braidwood st SE1
18 P 14   Bramber rd W14
24 Z 10   Bramcote gro SE16
19 J 13   Bramerton st SW3
18 Y 8   Bramham gdns SW5
9 G 9   Bramley rd W11
9 G 6   Bramley st W10
7 G 4   Branch pl N1
23 D 9   Brandar st SE17
23 C 7   Brandon st SE17
23 C 7   Brandon st SE17
22 R 10   Brangton rd SE11
17 J 20   Branksea st SW6
2 V 30   Bransdale clo NW6
8 S 18   Bratley st E1

2 O 16	Bravington pl W9	
2 O 16	Bravington rd W9	
2 O 11	Bravington rd W9	
20 O 8	Bray pl SW3	
6 S 2	Brayfield ter N1	
14 S 4	Breams bldgs EC4	
19 C 8	Brechin pl SW7	
17 L 16	Brecon rd W6	
16 U 10	Breezers hill E1	
11 D 20	Bremner rd SW7	
11 M 4	Brendon st W1	
21 A 2	Bressenden pl SW1	
23 F 10	Brettell st SE17	
13 D 9	Brewer st W1	
21 D 1	Brewers grn SW1	
6 X 17	Brewhouse yd EC1	
9 A 1	Brewster gdns W10	
14 S 8	Brick ct EC4	
16 P 2	Brick la E1	
12 W 15	Brick st W1	
14 W 6	Bride la EC4	
14 W /	Bridewell pl EC4	
14 Y 19	Bridford ms W1	
17 A 8	Bridge av W6	
20 Y 6	Bridge pl SW1	
13 K 18	Bridge st SW1	
17 A 9	Bridge view W6	
21 L 12	Bridgefoot SE1	
6 O 2	Bridgeman rd N1	
7 A 20	Bridgewater sq EC1	
5 D 9	Bridgeway st NW1	
13 C 9	Bridle la W1	
7 F 6	Bridport pl N1	
7 F 8	Bridport pl N1	
10 U 5	Bridstow pl W2	
23 20	Brisbane st SE5E	
6 W 19	Briset st EC1	
2 Z 19	Bristol gdns W9	
3 A 19	Bristol gdns W9	
2 Z 19	Bristol ms W9	
3 A 19	Bristol ms W9	
18 X 19	Britannia rd SW6	
6 Y 4	Britannia row N1	
6 N 12	Britannia st WC1	
7 E 12	Britannia wlk N1	
13 H 2	British Museum WC1	
19 J 10	Britten st SW3	
6 W 19	Britton st EC1	
22 T 18	Brixton rd SW9	
13 L 6	Broad ct WC2	
15 J 2	Broad st bldgs EC2	
15 H 1	Broad st Stn	
6 V 19	Broad yd EC1	
12 X 9	Broadbent st W1	
3 H 20	Broadley st NW8	
3 L 18	Broadley ter NW1	
12 S 2	Broadstone pl W1	
14 U 12	Broadwall SE1	
8 V 5	Broadway mkt E8	
13 F 20	Broadway W1	
13 C 8	Broadwick st W1	
23 C 1	Brockham st SE1	
23 K 16	Brockworth clo SE15	
24 P 10	Brodie st SE1	
8 R 4	Broke wlk E8	
6 U 7	Bromfield st N1	
5 A 19	Bromley pl W1	
20 N 1	Brompton pl SW3	
12 O 19	Brompton rd SW3	
19 K 3	Brompton rd SW3	
19 K 2	Brompton sq SW3	
1 K 2	Brondesbury pk NW6	
2 U 6	Brondesbury rd NW6	
17 J 19	Bronsart rd SW6	
2 U 7	Bronsesbury vills NW6	
23 C 10	Bronti clo SE17	
22 X 5	Brook dri SE11	
22 T 3	Brook dri SE11	
17 E 4	Brook grn W6	
11 E 8	Brook Ms north W2	

12 Y 7	Brook st W1	
11 H 9	Brook st W2	
14 T 2	Brooke st EC1	
14 T 1	Brooks mkt EC1	
12 X 8	Brooks ms W1	
1 L 6	Brooksville av NW6	
18 O 19	Brookville rd SW6	
23 D 19	Broome way SE5	
21 L 19	Brough clo SW8	
21 K 19	Brough st SW8	
8 T 3	Brougham rd E8	
12 V 7	Brown Hart gdns W1	
3 D 18	Browning clo W9	
6 O 17	Brownlow ms WC1	
8 R 3	Brownlow rd E8	
14 P 2	Brownlow st WC1	
15 K 5	Browns bldgs EC3	
12 N 4	Browns st W1	
3 M 7	Broxwood way NW8	
16 N 2	Brune st E1	
15 L 18	Brunswick ct SE1	
10 W 15	Brunswick gdns W8	
12 P 5	Brunswick ms W1	
7 F 14	Brunswick pl N1	
5 L 17	Brunswick sq WCC1	
16 N 1	Brushfield st E1	
15 L 1	Brushfield st E1	
12 Y 10	Bruton la W1	
12 Y 9	Bruton pl W1	
12 Y 10	Bruton st W1	
1 A 1	Bryan av NW10	
12 3	Bryanston Ms east W1	
12 O 3	Bryanston Ms west W1	
12 N 3	Bryanston pl W1	
12 O 4	Bryanston sq W1	
12 R 6	Bryanston st W1	
13 J 10	Brydges pl WC2	
5 L 4	Brydon wk N1	
1 A 9	Buchanan gdns NW10	
11 H 10	Buck Hill wlk W2	
4 Y 2	Buck st NW1	
8 T 14	Buckfast st E2	
8 Y 17	Buckhurst st E1	
13 L 12	Buckingham arcade WC2	
23 C 1	Buckingham ga SW1	
13 A 19	Buckingham Palace SW1	
20 X 6	Buckingham Palace rd SW1	
12 X 18	Buckingham Palace gdns SW1	
12 Z 19	Buckingham Palace SW1	
13 L 11	Buckingham st WC2	
7 G 9	Buckland st N1	
16 R 5	Buckle st E1	
2 P 2	Buckley rd NW6	
13 H 4	Bucknall st WC2	
2 N 13	Buckner st W10	
21 H 7	Bulinga st SW1	
13 L 9	Bull Inn ct WC2	
24 S 19	Buller clo SE15	
1 G 13	Buller rd NW10	
19 L 5	Bulls gdns SW3	
10 S 12	Bulmer ms W11	
12 V 3	Bulstrode pl W1	
12 V 3	Bulstrode st W1	
9 D 15	Bulwer st W12	
16 Y 7	Bunch st E1	
7 D 16	Bunhill row EC1	
21 F 10	Buonaparte mews SW1	
23 E 2	Burbage clo SE1	
14 T 20	Burdett st SE1	
24 N 9	Burgandy st SE1	
23 F 3	Burge st SE1	
23 E 2	Burge st SE1	
6 Z 8	Burgh st N1	
14 Y 7	Burgon st EC4	
13 M 8	Burleigh st WC2	

13 A 11	Burlington arc W1	
2 S 17	Burlington clo W9	
13 A 11	Burlington gdns W1	
22 X 2	Burman st SE1	
19 D 19	Burnaby st SW10	
19 B 20	Burnaby st SW10	
11 K 1	Burne st NW1	
22 N 10	Burnett st SE11	
19 L 10	Burnsall st SW3	
18 R 19	Burnthwaite rd SW6	
14 X 13	Burrell st SE1	
14 W 16	Burrows ms SE1	
1 C 12	Burrows rd NW10	
15 K 15	Bursar st SE1	
15 K 1	Burslem st E1	
16 U 6	Burslem st E1	
23 F 11	Burton gro SE17	
20 V 6	Burton mews SW1	
5 H 15	Burton pl WC1	
2 R 2	Burton rd NW6	
5 H 15	Burton st WC1	
16 X 6	Burwell clo E1	
11 L 5	Burwood pl W2	
15 K 5	Bury ct EC3	
13 K 2	Bury pl WC1	
15 K 5	Bury st EC3	
13 C 13	Bury st SW1	
19 J 8	Bury wlk SW3	
8 W 5	Bush rd E8	
16 T 14	Bushell st E1	
17 F 6	Bute gdns W6	
19 F 6	Bute st SW7	
17 E 8	Butterwick W6	
7 G 12	Buttesland st N1	
8 R 18	Buxton st E1	
16 Y 14	BVrewhouse la E1	
5 F 18	Byng pl WC1	
8 S 4	Byron clo E8	
15 L 10	Byward st EC3	
20 N 9	Bywater st SW3	
13 A 3	Bywell pl W1	

C

11 K 2	Cabbell st NW1	
16 X 8	Cable st E1	
23 C 11	Cadiz st SE17	
20 P 5	Cadogan ga SW3	
20 P 6	Cadogan gdns SW3	
20 R 2	Cadogan la SW1	
20 S 3	Cadogan la SW1	
20 R 1	Cadogan pl SW1	
20 O 4	Cadogan sq SW1	
20 N 7	Cadogan st SW3	
7 M 11	Caesar st E2	
8 O 13	Cahambord st E2	
2 N 15	Caird st W10	
17 G 3	Caithness rd W14	
22 W 18	Calberwell New rd SE5	
9 C 3	Calderon pl W10	
23 E 16	Caldew st SE5	
22 R 20	Caldwell st SW9	
19 J 9	Cale st SW3	
15 B 17	Caleb st SE1	
5 L 10	Caledonia st N1	
5 M 9	Caledonian rd N1	
6 N 4	Caledonian rd N1	
2 O 1	Callcott rd NW6	
10 T 13	Callcott st W8	
19 E 13	Callow st SW3	
23 K 13	Calmington rd SE5	
6 O 10	Calshot st N1	
6 P 16	Calthorpe st WC1	
7 M 14	Calvert av E2	
4 T 3	Calvert st NW1	
8 N 18	Calvin st E1	
5 L 4	Cambert wk N1	
23 C 17	Camberwell rd SE5	
9 L 6	Camborne ms W11	
18 Z 20	Cambria st SW6	
2 V 7	Cambridge av NW6	

13 G 7 Cambridge cir WC2
8 W 9 Cambridge cres E2
4 Y 15 Cambridge Ga ms NW1
4 X 15 Cambridge ga NW1
2 V 9 Cambridge gdns NW6
9 K 4 Cambridge gdns W10
17 A 7 Cambridge gro W6
8 Y 5 Cambridge Heath rd E2
10 Z 19 Cambridge pl W8
2 V 10 Cambridge rd NW6
2 U 12 Cambridge rd NW6
11 K 5 Cambridge sq W2
20 Y 8 Cambridge st SW1
21 A 10 Cambridge st SW1
4 Y 14 Cambridge Ter ms NW1
4 X 14 Cambridge ter NW1
24 N 20 Camden gro SE15
5 A 6 Camden High st NW1
4 Y 2 Camden High st NW1
4 W 1 Camden Lock pl NW1
6 V 8 Camden pas N1
5 A 2 Camden rd NW1
5 A 2 Camden st NW1
4 Z 1 Camden st NW1
6 X 7 Camden wlk N1
21 J 20 Camellia st SW8
19 E 14 Camera pl SW10
16 X 4 Cameron pl E1
24 V 6 Camilla rd SE16
8 N 16 Camlet st E2
5 E 5 Camley st NW1
15 K 4 Camomile st EC3
3 E 19 Campbell st W2
10 V 16 Campden gro W8
10 S 14 Campden Hill gnds W8
10 R 13 Campden Hill pl W11
10 T 15 Campden Hill rd W8
10 R 14 Campden Hill sq W8
10 S 16 Campden hill W8
10 U 16 Campden Ho clo W8
10 U 14 Campden st W8
16 O 6 Camperdown st E1
24 U 13 Canal gro SE15
23 E 15 Canal st SE5
7 G 3 Canal wlk N1
13 A 1 Candover st W1
11 A 20 Canning pas W8
11 B 20 Canning pl ms W8
13 K 18 Cannon row SW1
15 A 7 Cannon St rd E1
16 W 9 Cannon St rd E1
15 D 10 Cannon st sta EC4
7 B 5 Canon st N1
6 Y 1 Canonbury vlls N1
8 W 13 Canrobert st E2
22 Y 8 Canterbury pl SE17
2 T 9 Canterbury rd NW6
2 S 10 Canterbury ter NW6
14 Z 13 Canvey st SE1
12 S 19 Caperners clo SW1
5 D 19 Capper st WC1
10 S 4 Caradoc clo W2
4 Z 19 Carburton st W1
22 S 10 Cardigan st SE11
23 F 3 Cardinal Bourne st SE1
15 A 11 Cardinal Cap all SE1
24 W 18 Cardine ms SE15
5 B 13 Cardington st NW1
21 E 7 Carey pl SW1
14 R 5 Carey st WC2
15 M 7 Carlisle av EC3
14 R 20 Carlisle la SE1
22 P 1 Carlisle la SW1

21 A 3 Carlisle pl SW1
1 L 5 Carlisle rd NW6
13 E 5 Carlisle st W1
12 V 9 Carlos pl W1
5 A 7 Carlow st NW1
13 E 14 Carlton gdns SW1
24 X 20 Carlton gro SE15
3 C 6 Carlton hill NW8
2 Z 9 Carlton hill NW8
13 G 13 Carlton House ter SW1
13 E 12 Carlton st NW1
20 R 1 Carlton Tower pl SW1
2 S 10 Carlton vale NW6
19 G 12 Carlyle sq SW3
10 V 17 Carmel ct W8
14 V 8 Carmelite st EC4
13 B 8 Carnaby st W1
6 O 6 Carnegie st N1
6 N 1 Carnoustie dr N1
5 A 4 Carol st NW1
10 Y 10 Caroline clo W2
7 L 12 Caroline gdns E2
10 Y 10 Caroline Pl ms W2
10 Y 9 Caroline pl W2
20 T 6 Caroline ter SW1
12 W 10 Carpenter st W1
20 U 17 Carriage Dr east SW11
20 V 15 Carriage Dr north SW11
20 N 19 Carriage dr west SW11
12 X 14 Carrington st W1
22 O 17 Carroun rd SW8
14 Y 7 Carter la EC4
23 B 11 Carter pl SE17
22 Z 12 Carter st SE17
23 A 12 Carter st SE17
13 F 19 Carteret st SW1
6 Z 20 Carthusian st EC1
13 M 10 Carting la WC2
5 H 14 Cartwright gdns WC1
16 P 10 Cartwright st E1
8 Y 17 Caslon pl E1
23 E 18 Caspian st SE5
18 U 20 Cassidy rd SW5
16 S 1 Casson st E1
3 A 18 Castellain rd W9
2 X 15 Castellain rd W9
14 Z 9 Castle Baynard st EC4
21 B 1 Castle la SW1
4 X 1 Castlehaven rd NW1
12 N 3 Castlereagh st W1
17 M 11 Castletown rd W14
18 N 10 Castletown rd W14
8 V 5 Cat & Mutton bridge E8
23 G 7 Catesby st SE17
16 X 18 Cathay st SE16
19 A 13 Cathcart rd SW10
14 Z 5 Cathedral pl EC4
15 E 13 Cathedral st SE1
13 B 20 Catherine pl SW1
14 N 8 Catherine st WC2
15 K 2 Catherine Wheel all EC2
13 B 15 Catherine Wheel yd SW1
24 U 10 Catlin st SE16
11 M 3 Cato st W1
24 O 17 Cator st SE15
13 M 2 Catton st WC1
21 G 8 Causton st SW1
19 O 12 Cavaye pl SW10
16 Y 4 Cavell st E1
3 G 11 Cavendish av NW8
3 G 12 Cavendish clo NW8
15 K 3 Cavendish ct EC2
12 Y 1 Cavendish ms north W1

12 Y 1 Cavendish ms south W1
12 Y 3 Cavendish pl W1
12 Y 4 Cavendish sq W1
7 E 9 Cavendish st N1
20 N 13 Caversham st SW3
9 B 4 Caverswall st W12
4 T 3 Cavert st NW1
9 E 16 Caxton rd W12
21 D 1 Caxton st SW1
7 D 13 Cayton pl EC1
7 D 14 Cayton st EC1
13 H 10 Cecil ct WC2
18 W 19 Cedarne rd SW6
10 Y 3 Celbridge ms W2
22 R 1 Centaur st SE1
20 R 19 Central av SW11
14 W 2 Central mkts EC1
6 Z 12 Central st EC1
7 A 16 Central st EC1
8 W 9 Centre st E2
8 Z 17 Cephas st E1
17 J 2 Ceylon rd W14
6 U 11 Chadwell st EC1
21 F 3 Chadwick st SW1
4 P 18 Chagford st NW1
6 R 8 Chalbury wlk N1
4 R 3 Chalcot cres NW1
4 S 2 Chalcot rd NW1
4 S 1 Chalcot sq NW1
17 L 17 Chaldon rd SW6
17 G 8 Chalkhill rd W6
18 O 11 Challoner cres W14
18 O 11 Challoner st W14
5 D 8 Chalton st NW1
16 P 8 Chamber st E1
4 P 1 Chamberlain st NW1
1 D 7 Chamberlayne rd NW10
1 B 1 Chambers la NW10
16 T 18 Chambers st SE16
14 X 14 Chancel st SE1
17 C 10 Chancellors rd W6
17 D 11 Chancellors rd W6
17 C 11 Chancellors st W6
14 R 3 Chancery la WC2
16 X 12 Chandler st E1
13 K 10 Chandos pl WC2
12 Y 3 Chandos st W1
6 Y 6 Chantry st N1
15 E 17 Chapel ct SE1
6 S 8 Chapel mkt N1
6 T 8 Chapel pl N1
12 X 5 Chapel pl W1
10 W 10 Chapel side W2
11 K 2 Chapel st NW1
12 V 19 Chapel st SW1
14 V 17 Chaplin clo SE1
16 X 8 Chapman st E1
22 Y 12 Chapter rd SE17
21 E 7 Chapter st SW1
9 G 18 Charecroft way W12
13 G 8 Charing Cross rd WC2
13 K 9 Charlbert st NW8
3 J 9 Charles la NW8
13 E 12 Charles st SW11
12 W 12 Charles st W1
23 C 7 Charleston st SE17
17 M 11 Charleville rd SE26
18 N 10 Charleville rd W14
5 C 20 Charlotte ms W1
13 D 2 Charlotte pl W1
7 K 14 Charlotte rd EC2
13 D 2 Charlotte st W1
5 C 20 Charlotte st W1
6 R 6 Charlotte ter N1
6 W 7 Charlton pl N1
21 C 8 Charlwood pl SW1
21 B 9 Charlwood st SW1
5 E 8 Charrington st NW1
7 G 13 Chart st N1
6 Y 19 Charterhouse sq EC1
14 W 1 Charterhouse st EC1

6 Y 20 Charterhouse st EC1
2 R 5 Charteris rd NW6
23 F 5 Chatham st SE17
15 B 6 Cheapside EC2
1 B 5 Chelmsford sq NW10
17 J 12 Chelmsford st
20 U 11 Chelsea Br rd SW1
20 W 13 Chelsea br SW1
20 R 14 Chelsea emb SW3
19 L 15 Chelsea Embankment gdns SW3
19 K 12 Chelsea Manor gdns SW3
19 L 12 Chelsea Manor st SW3
19 F 14 Chelsea Pk gdns SW3
19 H 10 Chelsea sq SW3
20 P 9 Cheltenham ter SW3
5 J 10 Cheney rd NW1
5 E 18 Chenies ms WC1
5 F 8 Chenies pl NW1
5 E 20 Chenies st WC1
18 W 1 Cheniston gdns W8
18 X 1 Cheniston gdns W8
10 T 8 Chepstow cr4es W11
10 U 7 Chepstow pl W2
10 U 4 Chepstow rd W2
10 R 9 Chepstow vlls W11
7 D 18 Chequer st EC1
7 G 9 Cherbury st N1
16 W 19 Cherry Gdn st SE16
20 S 2 Chesham clo SW1
20 S 2 Chesham pl SW1
20 S 3 Chesham st SW1
20 S 1 Chesham st SW1
8 S 16 Cheshire st E2
18 P 13 Chesson rd W14
4 X 13 Chester Clo north NW1
4 X 13 Chester Clo south NW1
12 W 20 Chester clo SW1
4 X 14 Chester ga NW1
12 W 20 Chester ms SW1
4 X 11 Chester pl NW1
4 V 13 Chester rd NW1
20 T 7 Chester row SW1
20 U 5 Chester row SW1
20 W 3 Chester Sq ms SW1
20 V 4 Chester sq SW1
12 W 20 Chester st SW1
22 T 7 Chester way SE11
21 G 12 Chester Wharf SW1
12 W 13 Chesterfield gdns W1
12 W 12 Chesterfield hill W1
12 W 13 Chesterfield st W1
9 H 3 Chesterton rd W10
18 R 15 Chestnut all SW6
18 R 15 Chestnut ct SW6
23 E 2 Chettle clo
19 L 1 Cheval pl SW7
1 G 9 Chevening rd NW6
19 M 14 Cheyne gdns SW3
20 O 13 Cheyne pl SW3
19 K 15 Cheyne row SW3
19 F 17 Cheyne wlk SW10
19 L 15 Cheyne wlk SW3
19 K 16 Cheyne wlk SW3
14 O 16 Chicheley st SE1
2 U 9 Chichester rd NW6
2 Z 20 Chichester rd W9
14 R 5 Chichester rents WC2
21 D 11 Chichester st SW1
16 R 1 Chicksand st E1
16 X 10 Chigwell hill E1
18 V 6 Childs pl SW5
18 V 6 Childs st SW5
18 V 6 Childs wlk SW5

4 S 19 Chiltern st W1
12 S 2 Chiltern st W1
8 R 15 Chilton st E2
11 E 6 Chilworth ms W2
11 C 6 Chilworth st W2
2 U 19 Chippenham ms W9
2 T 18 Chippenham rd W9
7 E 20 Chiswell st EC1
5 C 20 Chitty st W1
16 Y 13 Choppins ct E1
1 J 3 Christchurch av NW6
20 N 13 Christchurch st SW3
20 O 13 Christchurch ter SW3
16 U 7 Christian st E1
7 J 17 Christina st EC2
5 G 13 Christopher pl NW1
7 G 19 Christopher st EC2
22 U 19 Chryssel rd SW9
1 E 1 Chudleigh rd NW6
23 H 14 Chumleigh st SE5
10 W 16 Church clo W8
14 T 7 Church ct WC2
14 X 7 Church entry EC4
22 U 20 Church Manor Est SW9
13 D 11 Church pl SW1
18 X 19 Church row SW6
3 H 20 Church st NW8
3 G 20 Church st W2
21 A 12 Churchill Gardens Est SW1
21 B 12 Churchill Gdns rd SW1
20 Z 12 Churchill gdns SW1
5 F 12 Churchway NW1
22 X 5 Churchyard row SE11
21 B 7 Churton pl SW1
21 B 8 Churton st SW1
16 Z 13 Cinnamon st E1
12 N 1 Circus ms W1
3 G 10 Circus rd NW8
2 X 20 Cirencester st W2
6 Y 10 City Gdn row N1
7 C 12 City rd EC1
6 Y 11 City rd EC1
20 O 4 Clabon ms SW1
10 V 10 Clanricarde gdns W2
22 R 18 Clapham rd SW9
9 M 6 Clare gdns W11
7 B 1 Clare la N1
14 O 6 Clare mkt WC2
8 X 9 Clare st E2
8 V 10 Claredale st E2
8 T 11 Claremont clo N1
2 N 10 Claremont rd W9
6 S 10 Claremont sq N1
4 P 16 Clarence gate NW1
4 Z 14 Clarence gdns NW1
5 J 9 Clarence pas NW1
2 O 2 Clarence rd NW6
4 O 16 Clarence ter NW1
11 K 8 Clarendon clo W2
9 L 11 Clarendon cross W11
3 C 18 Clarendon gdns W9
11 K 8 Clarendon ms W2
11 K 8 Clarendon pl W2
10 N 13 Clarendon rd W11
9 K 8 Clarendon rd W11
20 Y 10 Clarendon st SW1
21 A 8 Clarendon st SW1
3 D 17 Clarendon ter W9
19 D 7 Clareville gro SW7
19 D 7 Clareville st SW7
12 X 12 Clarges ms W1
12 Y 13 Clarges st W1
8 N 4 Clarissa st E8
16 Z 3 Clark st E1

12 V 1 Clarkes pl W1
15 J 4 Clarks pl EC3
16 Z 13 Clave st E1
17 A 14 Clavering av SW13
21 C 12 Claverton st SW1
17 H 11 Claxton gro W6
12 R 2 Clay st W1
17 G 13 Claybrook rd W6
22 R 16 Claylands pl SW8
22 T 13 Clayton st SE11
2 Y 19 Clearwell dr W9
22 U 10 Cleaver sq SE11
22 U 10 Cleaver st SE11
16 Y 13 Clegg st E13
18 O 15 Clem Attlee ct SW6
1 E 2 Clement clo NW6
24 V 3 Clements rd SE16
12 O 5 Clenston ms W1
7 G 16 Clere pl EC2
7 G 17 Clere st EC2
6 V 17 Clerkenwell clo EC1
6 V 17 Clerkenwell grn EC1
6 W 17 Clerkenwell rd EC1
11 B 6 Cleveland gdns W2
5 B 19 Cleveland ms W1
13 D 13 Cleveland pl SW1
7 F 2 Cleveland rd N1
13 B 15 Cleveland row SW1
11 B 7 Cleveland sq W2
4 Z 18 Cleveland st W1
5 A 19 Cleveland st W1
11 C 4 Cleveland ter W2
1 C 9 Clifford gdns NW10
13 A 9 Clifford st W1
24 Z 18 Clifton cres SE15
3 B 18 Clifton gdns W9
3 C 5 Clifton hill NW8
2 Y 8 Clifton hill NW8
11 H 7 Clifton pl W2
3 D 17 Clifton rd W9
7 H 19 Clifton st EC2
3 A 20 Clifton vlls W9
24 Z 20 Clifton way SE15
15 D 12 Clink st SE1
5 A 20 Clipstone st W1
4 Z 20 Clipstone st W1
20 S 6 Cliveden pl SW1
22 Y 6 Clock pl SE17
7 C 6 Clock Tower ms N1
18 P 20 Clonmel rd SW6
14 Y 1 Cloth ct EC1
14 Y 2 Cloth fair EC1
15 A 1 Cloth st EC1
15 L 4 Clothier st E1
6 T 6 Cloudesley pl N1
6 T 5 Cloudesley rd N1
6 T 4 Cloudesley sq N1
6 T 5 Cloudeslcy st N1
20 O 13 Clover ms SW3
8 N 16 Club row E2
18 S 8 Cluny ms SW5
23 J 1 Cluny pl SE1
10 P 5 Clydesdale rd W11
8 U 8 Coate st E2
15 M 3 Cobb st E1
22 O 20 Cobbett st SW8
14 X 7 Cobbs ct EC4
24 N 11 Cobourg rd SE5
5 C 14 Cobourg st NW1
3 H 10 Cochrane st NW8
15 L 3 Cock hill E1
14 X 3 Cock la EC1
13 F 19 Cockpit steps SW1
6 O 19 Cockpit yd WC1
13 G 13 Cockspur ct SW1
13 H 13 Cockspur st SW1
8 P 18 Code st E1
10 N 7 Codrington ms W11
14 T 13 Coin st SE1
16 T 4 Coke st E1
19 A 7 Colbeck ms SW7
6 S 17 Coldbath sq EC1
15 D 19 Cole st SE1

18 Z 7 Colebeck ms SW5
6 X 7 Colebrooke row N1
18 Y 12 Coleherne ms SW10
18 X 11 Coleherne rd SW10
7 B 4 Coleman fields N1
23 K 18 Coleman rd SE5
23 H 17 Coleman rd SE5
15 E 5 Coleman st EC2
3 B 2 Coleridge gdns NW6
17 H 7 Colet gdns W14
6 P 17 Coley st WC1
6 V 1 College cross N1
5 D 5 College gro NW1
5 C 4 College pl NW1
1 B 8 College rd NW10
24 U 2 Collett rd SE16
6 N 9 Collier st N1
18 Z 7 Collingham gdns SW5
18 Y 6 Collingham pl SW5
8 X 17 Collingwood st E1
6 X 5 Collins yd N1
15 A 19 Collinson st SE1
8 R 16 Colman clo E2
22 W 2 Colnbrook st SE1
14 W 15 Colombo st SE1
5 K 18 Colonnade WC1
4 Y 15 Colosseum ter NW1
8 P 12 Columbia rd E2
10 P 6 Colville gdns W11
10 R 6 Colville ms W11
13 D 2 Colville pl W1
10 P 5 Colville rd W11
10 R 7 Colville rd W11
10 O 5 Colville Sq ms W11
10 O 6 Colville sq W11
10 P 6 Colville ter W11
17 E 14 Colwith rd W6
23 B 8 Colworth gro SE17
23 B 20 Comber gro SE5
17 M 10 Comeragh ms W14
18 N 10 Comeragh rd W14
17 L 11 Comeragh rd W14
16 U 5 Commercial rd E1
16 O 2 Commercial st E1
23 M 20 Commercial way SE15
24 T 18 Commercial way SE15
10 S 20 Commonwealth institute W8
4 Z 14 Compton clo NW1
5 K 15 Compton pl WC1
1 G 13 Compton rd NW10
6 X 16 Compton st EC1
23 H 6 Comus pl SE17
14 P 14 Concert Hall appr SE1
13 K 8 Conduit ct WC2
11 F 7 Conduit ms W2
11 F 6 Conduit pas W2
11 G 6 Conduit pl W2
13 A 8 Conduit st W1
12 Z 9 Conduit st W1
23 J 7 Congreve st SE17
1 L 17 Conlan st W10
11 L 7 Connaught clo W2
12 N 7 Connaught ms W2
12 N 7 Connaught pl W2
12 N 6 Connaught sq W2
11 M 6 Connaught st W2
11 M 7 Connaught sw W2
14 U 16 Cons st SE1
12 Y 17 Constitution hill SW1
23 C 7 Content st SE17
5 A 18 Conway st W1
22 V 14 Cooks rd SE17
2 O 15 Coomassie rd W9
6 Y 10 Coombs st N1
5 G 9 Coopers la NW1
24 P 10 Coopers rd SE1
15 M 8 Coopers row EC3

18 U 2 Cope pl W8
6 S 6 Copenhagen st N1
5 L 5 Copenhagen st N1
6 Z 4 Copford wlk N1
7 A 3 Copford wlk N1
14 Z 16 Copperfield st SE1
15 A 16 Copperfield st SE1
13 J 2 Coptic st WC1
14 T 18 Coral st SE1
5 J 17 Coram st WC1
8 O 19 Corbet pl E1
8 X 7 Corbridge cres E2
8 X 15 Corfield st E2
13 A 10 Cork St ms W1
13 A 10 Cork st W1
11 J 1 Corlett st NW1
15 G 6 Cornhill EC3
9 L 7 Cornwall cres W11
18 Z 3 Cornwall gdns SW7
19 A 3 Cornwall gdns SW7
18 Y 3 Cornwall gdns wlk SW7
19 A 3 Cornwall Ms south SW7
18 X 2 Cornwall Ms west SW7
14 T 14 Cornwall rd SE1
16 X 8 Cornwall st E1
4 S 18 Cornwall ter NW1
7 J 13 Coronet st N1
6 U 16 Corporation row EC1
7 G 13 Corsham st N1
5 L 20 Cosmo pl WC1
22 S 2 Cosser st SE1
3 L 20 Cosway st NW1
23 C 7 Cotham st SE17
23 H 18 Cottage grn SE5
19 J 2 Cottage pl SW3
18 Z 1 Cottesmore gdns W8
19 A 1 Cottesmore gdns W8
22 V 9 Cottington st SE11
7 M 12 Cottons gdns E2
20 O 8 Coulson st SW3
17 A 2 Coulter rd W6
23 A 20 Councillor st SE5
15 E 15 Counter ct SE1
23 D 3 County st SE1
23 C 3 County st SE1
22 S 10 Courtenay sq SE11
22 S 10 Courtenay st SE11
18 Z 6 Courtfield gdns SW5
18 Y 6 Courtfield gdns SW5
19 A 6 Courtfield rd SW7
10 S 5 Courtnell st W2
13 L 8 Covent gdn WC2
10 N 6 Covent gdns W11
2 V 7 Coventry clo NW6
8 Y 17 Coventry rd E1
8 Y 15 Coventry rd E1
13 E 10 Coventry st W1
9 A 16 Coverdale rd W12
8 T 20 Coverley clo E1
23 J 13 Cowan st SE5
6 X 20 Cowcross st EC1
6 N 3 Cowdenbeath pth N1
22 U 20 Cowley rd SW14
21 J 1 Cowley st SW1
7 G 15 Cowper st EC2
9 F 2 Cowper ter W10
14 Z 3 Coxs ct EC1
16 N 18 Coxson pl SE1
17 F 17 Crabtree la SW6
13 J 13 Craigs ct SW1
23 F 6 Crail row SE17
13 H 9 Crambourne st WC2
12 U 2 Cramer st W1
22 Z 8 Crampton st SE17
22 Z 7 Crampton st SE17
8 T 18 Cranberry st E1
13 H 9 Cranbourne all WC2

14 U 5 Crane ct EC4
5 C 9 Cranleigh st NW1
19 D 9 Cranley gdns SW7
19 D 9 Cranley ms SW7
19 F 7 Cranley pl SW7
22 U 18 Cranmer rd SW9
24 Y 10 Cranswick rd SE16
7 F 14 Cranwood st EC1
11 C 9 Craven Hill gdn W2
11 C 8 Craven Hill ms W2
11 D 8 Craven hill W2
13 K 12 Craven pas WC2
11 D 7 Craven rd W2
13 K 12 Craven st WC2
11 D 8 Craven ter W2
12 O 1 Crawford ms W1
6 T 17 Crawford pas EC1
11 L 3 Crawford pl W1
12 N 2 Crawford st W1
23 K 3 Creasy est SE1
1 E 6 Crediton rd NW10
24 Y 10 Credon rd SE16
15 L 6 Creechurch la EC3
15 L 6 Creechurch pl EC3
14 Y 6 Creed la EC4
17 J 16 Crefeld clo W6
1 H 8 Creighton rd NW6
7 M 10 Cremer st E2
19 G 16 Cremorne est SW10
19 D 20 Cremorne gdns SW10
19 E 19 Cremorne rd SW10
19 L 5 Crescent pl SW3
7 A 17 Crescent row EC1
16 N 9 Crescent the EC3
19 B 9 Cresswell gdns SW5
19 C 10 Cresswell pl SW10
5 K 12 Crestfield st WC1
22 S 19 Crewdson rd SW9
22 X 7 Cricketers ct SE11
23 L 3 Crimscott st SE1
21 F 20 Crimsworth rd SW8
5 L 7 Crinan st N1
21 C 17 Cringle st SW8
17 C 11 Crisp rd W6
15 M 1 Crispin st E1
16 R 10 Crofts st E1
5 K 14 Cromer st WC1
3 E 19 Crompton st W2
18 S 5 Cromwell cres W8
19 H 4 Cromwell gdns SW7
9 D 20 Cromwell gro W6
19 F 5 Cromwell ms SW7
19 G 4 Cromwell pl SW7
18 X 5 Cromwell rd SW5
19 C 5 Cromwell rd SW7
7 J 10 Crondall st N1
7 E 10 Cropley st N1
15 F 18 Crosby row SE1
15 J 5 Crosby sq EC3
12 U 2 Cross Keys clo W1
15 K 10 Cross la EC3
6 Y 3 Cross st N1
15 M 8 Crosswall EC3
16 N 7 Crosswall SE3
8 U 3 Croston st E8
16 W 9 Crowder st E1
13 M 7 Crown ct WC2
14 T 8 Crown Office row EC4
13 C 14 Crown pas SW1
23 B 18 Crown st SE5
5 B 8 Crowndale rd NW1
2 R 13 Croxley rd W9
2 P 16 Croyton pth W9
15 K 17 Crucifix la SE1
6 Y 6 Cruden st N1
6 R 11 Cruikshank st WC1
15 L 8 Crutched Friars EC3
6 O 14 Cubitt st WC1
8 X 16 Cudworth st E1
20 O 7 Culford gdns SW3
7 J 2 Culford rd N1

16 Z 20 Culling rd SE16
15 J 7 Cullum st EC3
24 Z 19 Culmore rd SE15
6 S 7 Culpepper st N1
12 S 9 Culross st W1
3 K 10 Culworth st NW8
17 M 5 Cumberland cres W14
6 R 12 Cumberland gdns WC1
12 N 5 Cumberland mans W1
4 Z 12 Cumberland mkt NW1
4 X 12 Cumberland pl NW1
21 A 11 Cumberland st SW1
20 Y 10 Cumberland st SW1
4 X 10 Cumberland Ter ms NW1
4 X 10 Cumberland ter NW1
6 O 9 Cumming st N1
23 H 14 Cunard st SE5
20 V 7 Cundy st SW1
3 F 16 Cunningham pl NW8
21 G 8 Cureton st SW1
14 S 4 Curistor st EC4
16 O 16 Curlew st SE1
7 K 14 Curtain rd EC2
23 M 4 Curtis st SE1
12 V 14 Curzon pl W1
12 W 13 Curzon st W1
14 U 17 Cut the SE1
3 F 20 Cuthbert st W2
15 L 4 Cutler st E1
8 O 16 Cygnet st E2
6 P 9 Cynthia st N1
5 C 19 Cypress pl W1
6 X 15 Cyrus st EC1

D

13 D 6 D'arblay st W1
20 S 5 D'Oyley st SW1
13 F 20 Dacre st SW1
1 E 10 Dagmar gdns NW10
6 X 3 Dagmar pas N1
6 X 3 Dagmar ter N1
9 L 6 Dale row W11
1 C 20 Dalgarno gdns W10
9 A 1 Dalgarno gdns W10
1 D 19 Dalgarno way W10
6 X 16 Dallington st EC1
23 L 20 Dalwood st SE5
19 C 19 Damer ter SW10
16 Y 4 Damien st E1
6 Y B Danbury st N1
23 M 16 Daniel gdns SE15
24 O 17 Daniel gdns SE15
13 F 9 Dansey pl W1
22 X 6 Dante rd SE11
19 L 9 Danube st SW3
19 H 15 Danvers st SW3
18 R 20 Darlan rd SW6
8 Y 19 Darling row E1
J 13 Darnley ter W11
2 N 12 Dart st W10
23 B 13 Dartford st SE17
10 S 4 Dartmouth clo W2
13 F 19 Dartmouth st SW1
23 G 5 Darwin st SE17
23 D 10 Date st SE17
16 T 2 Davenant st E1
3 K 20 Daventry st NW1
24 O 15 Davey st SE15
4 S 20 David ms W1
14 X 19 Davidge st SE1
21 J 18 Davidson gdns SW8
12 W 8 Davies ms W9
12 W 9 Davies st W1
17 K 17 Dawes rd SW6
18 P 18 Dawes rd SW6
23 F 8 Dawes st SE17

23 G 9 Dawes st SE17
10 U 9 Dawson pl W2
8 O 9 Dawson st W1
13 E 5 ddiadem ct W1
7 K 4 De Beauvoir cres N1
7 J 2 De Beauvoir rd N1
7 K 1 De Beauvoir sq N1
22 W 11 De Laune st SE17
11 A 19 De Vere gdns W8
11 A 20 De Vere ms W8
12 V 2 De Walden st W1
23 B 4 Deacon way SE17
8 B 4 Deal st E1
21 J 4 Dean Bradley st SW1
13 F 20 Dean Farrar st SW1
21 J 4 Dean Ryle st SW1
13 F 7 Dean st W1
21 J 3 Dean Stanley st SW1
21 J 3 Dean Trench st SW1
16 Z 6 Deancross st E1
12 U 13 Deanery ms W1
12 U 13 Deanery st W1
23 F 8 Deans bldgs SE17
14 Y 7 Deans ct EC4
12 X 4 Deans ms W1
13 H 20 Deans yd SW1
23 J 1 Decima st SE1
24 Y 10 Delaford rd SE16
18 N 16 Delaford st SW6
2 Y 20 Delamere ter W2
11 A 1 Delamere ter W2
4 X 6 Delancey st NW1
2 W 16 Delaware rd W9
5 L 5 Delhi st N1
19 Y 8 Dellow st E1
21 B 7 Dells ms SW1
17 H 15 Delorme st W6
8 S 12 Delta st E2
22 Y 10 Delverton rd SE17
10 R 8 Denbigh clo W11
21 B 9 Denbigh pl SW1
10 R 8 Denbigh rd W11
21 C 10 Denbigh st SW1
10 R 8 Denbigh ter W11
2 R 12 Denhome rd W3
13 E 9 Denman st W1
6 S 7 Denmark gro N1
13 G 5 Denmark pl WC2
2 R 9 Denmark rd NW6
13 H 5 Denmark st WC2
8 P 5 Denne ter E8
3 D 14 Denning clo NW8
22 U 8 Denny cres SE11
22 T 8 Denny st SE11
19 M 6 Denyer st SW3
23 F 16 Depot st SE5
13 K 17 Derby ga SW1
12 V 14 Derby st W1
8 U 14 Derbyshire st E2
7 K 15 Dereham pl EC2
8 V 4 Dericote st E8
12 X 6 Dering st W1
10 X 19 Derry st W8
2 X 20 Desborough st W2
23 E 3 Deverell st SE1
14 R 7 Devereux ct WC2
24 X 15 Devon st SE15
6 X 7 Devonia rtd N1
4 X 20 Devonshire clo W1
24 Y 16 Devonshire gro SE15
4 X 20 Devonshire Ms north W1
4 V 19 Devonshire Ms west W1
4 W 20 Devonshire Ms south W1
4 V 19 Devonshire Pl ms W1
4 V 19 Devonshire pl W1

15 K 3 Devonshire row EC2
4 Y 19 Devonshire row ms W1
15 L 3 Devonshire sq EC2
4 X 19 Devonshire st W1
11 C 7 Devonshire ter W2
6 S 7 Dewey rd N1
17 F 2 Dewhurst rd W14
F 4 Dewsbury gdns Worc Pk
23 L 19 Diamond st SE15
4 Z 17 Diana pl NW1
6 Z 3 Dibden st N1
23 C 1 Dicens sq SE1
6 S 6 Dignum st N1
20 P 14 Dilke st SW3
7 B 13 Dingley pl EC1
7 B 13 Dingley rd EC1
8 V 9 Dinmont st E2
17 L 15 Disbrowe rd W6
15 C 17 Disney pl SE1
15 C 17 Disney st SE1
8 O 11 Diss st E2
15 A 8 Distaff la EC4
17 E 11 Distillery la W6
17 D 12 Distillery rd W6
16 W 19 Dixons all SE16
1 A 1 Dobree av NW10
16 S 9 Dock st E1
16 P 18 Dockhead SE1
24 S 2 Dockley rd SE16
22 X 12 Doddington gro SE17
22 W 13 Doddington pl SE17
14 V 20 Dodson st SE1
14 P 1 Dog and Duck yd WC1
14 X 14 Dolben st SE1
22 P 11 Dolland st SE11
21 D 12 Dolphin sq SW1
6 N 20 Dombey st WC1
7 A 17 Domingo st EC1
15 G 1 Dominion st EC2
23 M 11 Domville gro SE5
2 P 6 Donaldson rd W6
6 R 9 Donegal st N1
19 L 5 Donne pl SW3
1 A 3 Donnington rd NW10
14 S 13 Doon st SE1
5 F 13 Doric way NW1
3 E 4 Dorman way NW8
14 T 1 Dorrington st EC1
14 V 7 Dorset bldgs EC4
4 O 19 Dorset clo NW1
20 W 1 Dorset ms SW1
21 F 9 Dorset rd SW8
21 M 18 Dorset rd SW8
22 P 19 Dorset rd SW8
14 V 7 Dorset ri EC4
4 O 18 Dorset sq NW1
12 S 1 Dorset st W1
6 N 17 Doughty ms WC1
6 O 17 Doughty st WC1
21 F 8 Douglas pth SW1
2 P 3 Douglas rd NW6
21 F 7 Douglas st SW1
10 Z 20 Douro pl W8
19 B 8 Dove ms SW5
8 T 7 Dove row E2
19 J 11 Dovehouse st Sw3
12 Z 11 Dover st W1
13 A 12 Dover st W1
2 N 11 Dowland st W10
23 J 18 Dowlas st SE5
17 A 8 Down pl W6
12 X 15 Down st W1
2 W 18 Downfield clo W9
7 E 2 Downham rd N1
13 J 16 Downing st SW1
6 T 4 Downrey st N1
15 B 16 Doyce st SE1
1 A 8 Doyle gdns NW10

23 A 13 Draco st SE17
19 K 6 Draycott av SW3
20 N 7 Draycott av SW3
20 N 7 Draycott pl SW3
20 O 6 Draycott ter SW3
2 P 16 Drayford clo W9
10 V 18 Drayson mews W8
19 B 9 Drayton gdns SW10
1 M 15 Droop st W10
1 J 14 Droop st W10
24 Y 17 Drover la SE15
15 L 16 Druid st SE1
16 O 19 Druid st SE1
5 E 12 Drummond cres NW1
21 F 10 Drummond ga SW1
24 W 1 Drummond rd SE16
16 W 20 Drummond rd SE16
5 C 14 Drummond st NW1
13 L 5 Drury la WC2
22 U 7 Dryden Ct Housing est SE11
22 V 6 Dryden ct SE11
13 L 6 Dryden st WC2
7 L 13 Drysdale st N1
9 A 5 Du Cane rd W12
8 P 14 Ducat st E2
12 X 2 Duchess ms W1
10 T 18 Duchess of Bedford's wlk W8
12 Y 2 Duchess st W1
14 T 12 Duchy st SE1
13 D 7 Duck la W1
2 N 8 Dudley st NW6
11 F 2 Dudley st W2
11 F 2 Dudley st W2
19 H 9 Dudmaston ms SW3
7 D 17 Dufferin av EC1
7 D 18 Dufferin st EC1
13 C 7 Dufours pl W1
12 V 17 Duke of Wellington pl SW1
13 D 12 Duke of York st SW1
15 G 13 Duke St hill SE1
13 C 12 Duke st St James SW1
10 V 17 Dukes la W8
12 U 4 Dukes ms W1
15 M 6 Dukes pl EC3
5 G 14 Dukes rd WC1
12 U 7 Duke st W1
9 J 8 Dulford st W11
4 T 1 Dumpton pl NW1
7 V 16 Dunbridge st E2
8 V 4 Duncan rd E8
6 V 8 Duncan st N1
6 W 9 Duncan ter N1
13 J 11 Duncannon st WC2
16 X 15 Dundee st E1
16 K 9 Dundela gdns Worc Pk
1 F 6 Dundonald rd NW10
16 S 1 Dunk st E1
7 M 9 Dunloe st E2
8 P 9 Dunloe st E2
24 P 3 Dunlop pl SE16
1 K 5 Dunmore rd NW6
7 A 3 Dunmow wlk N1
12 S 8 Dunraven st W1
17 E 3 Dunsany rd W14
4 V 20 Dunstable ms W1
2 P 1 Dunster gdns NW6
8 N 5 Dunston rd E8
7 M 4 Dunston st E8
24 O 5 Dunton rd SE1
23 M 8 Dunton rd SE1
12 R 18 Duplex ride SW1
8 S 11 Durant st E2
13 L 11 Durham Ho st WC2
20 O 11 Durham pl SW3
22 O 12 Durham st SE11
10 W 4 Durham ter W2

16 V 1 Durward st E1
8 W 20 Durward st E1
12 R 1 Durweston ms W1
12 P 1 Durweston st W1
14 T 3 Dyers bldgs EC1
2 N 1 Dyne rd NW6
13 H 3 Dyott st WC1
7 H 19 Dysart st EC2

E

6 W 20 Eagle ct EC1
14 O 2 Eagle st WC1
7 D 7 Eagle Wharf rd N1
3 L 9 Eamont st NW8
18 U 11 Eardley cres SW5
24 N 9 Earl cotts SE1
24 N 9 Earl rd SE1
7 H 20 Earl st EC2
13 J 6 Earlham st WC2
18 T 10 Earls Ct Exhibition bldg SW5
18 X 7 Earls Ct gdns SW5
18 T 2 Earls Ct rd W8
18 W 10 Earls Ct sq SW5
18 R 3 Earls ter W8
18 T 3 Earls wlk W8
5 M 3 Earlsferry way N1
1 A 11 Earlsmead rd NW10
6 W 13 Earlstoke st EC1
8 Y 5 Earlston gro E9
4 X 3 Early ms NW1
13 H 4 Earnshaw ct WC2
17 M 5 Earsby st W14
12 V 4 Easleys ms W1
14 U 5 East Harding st EC4
16 S 20 East la SE16
16 X 1 East Mount st E1
14 Z 1 East pas EC1
14 X 1 East Poultry av EC1
7 F 12 East rd N1
1 L 17 East row W1
16 R 11 East Smithfield E1
23 K 7 East st SE17
23 G 8 East st SE17
23 C 10 East st SE17
24 N 19 East Surrey gro SE15
16 P 6 East Tenter st E1
11 D 5 Eastbourne ms W2
11 D 5 Eastbourne ter W2
13 C 4 Eastcastle st W1
15 H 9 Eastcheap EC3
6 S 15 Easton st WC1
20 T 6 Eaton clo SW1
20 V 3 Eaton gate SW1
20 Y 2 Eaton la SW1
20 U 3 Eaton Ms north SW1
20 V 4 Eaton Ms south SW1
20 U 5 Eaton Ms west SW1
20 U 3 Eaton pl SW1
20 W 2 Eaton row SW1
20 U 3 Eaton sq SW1
20 T 5 Eaton Ter ms SW1
20 S 5 Eaton ter SW1
20 T 6 Eaton ter SW1
22 O 15 Ebbisham drive SE11
7 E 13 Ebenezer st N1
23 L 15 Ebley clo SE15
7 M 16 Ebor st E2
20 V 11 Ebury Br rd SW1
20 W 9 Ebury Br SW1
20 W 4 Ebury Ms east SW1
20 W 5 Ebury ms SW1
20 V 7 Ebury sq SW1
20 V 6 Ebury st SW1
7 B 2 Ecclesbourne rd N1

20 Y 5 Eccleston br SW1
20 V 2 Eccleston ms SW1
20 W 6 Eccleston ms SW1
20 Z 7 Eccleston Sq ms SW1
20 Z 7 Eccleston sq SW1
20 X 5 Eccleston st SW1
8 R 18 Eckersley st E1
6 R 7 Eckford st N1
2 U 18 Edbrooke rd W9
6 Z 4 Eder wlk N1
10 U 14 Edge st WW8
11 K 3 Edgware rd W2
3 F 19 Edgware rd W2
12 N 6 Edgware rd W2
4 U 2 Edis st NW1
18 N 8 Edith rd W14
17 J 6 Edith rd W14
8 R 7 Edith st E2
18 B 17 Edith ter SW10
18 O 8 Edith vlls W14
23 F 18 Edmund st SE5
6 N 6 Edward sq N1
18 R 3 Edwardes sq W8
12 T 6 Edwards ms W1
12 T 6 Edwards ms W1
6 N 6 Edwards sq N1
18 U 19 Effie pl SW6
18 U 19 Effie rd SW6
24 W 10 Egan way SE16
4 T 3 Egbert pl NW1
4 T 2 Egbert st NW1
19 L 4 Egerton cres SW3
19 L 3 Egerton Gdns ms SW3
1 C 5 Egerton gdns NW10
19 K 4 Egerton gdns SW3
19 L 3 Egerton pl SW3
19 K 3 Egerton ter SW3
23 C 5 Elba pl SE17
19 L 19 Elcho st SW11
24 V 18 Elcot av SE15
7 M 19 Elder st E1
19 A 2 Eldon rd W8
18 Z 2 Eldon rd W8
15 H 1 Eldon st EC2
22 Y 3 Elephant and Castle SE1
16 Z 17 Elephant la SE16
23 A 4 Elephant rd SE17
3 A 12 Elgin av W9
2 T 17 Elgin av W9
10 N 7 Elgin cres W11
9 L 8 Elgin cres W11
2 Z 12 Elgin Ms north W9
3 A 13 Elgin Ms south W9
9 M 5 Elgin ms W11
6 W 10 Elia st N1
22 S 16 Elias pl SE11
7 D 2 Elizabeth av N1
20 X 7 Elizabeth br SW1
3 D 17 Elizabeth clo W9
20 W 6 Elizabeth st SW1
2 O 20 Elkstone rd W10
17 F 15 Ellaline rd W6
16 T 7 Ellen st E1
22 W 20 Elliott rd SW9
22 X 4 Elliotts row SE11
20 R 4 Ellis st SW1
8 X 12 Ellsworth st E2
19 F 11 Elm Pk gdns SW10
19 F 12 Elm Pk la SW3
19 E 14 Elm Pk rd SW3
19 F 10 Elm pl SW7
6 P 17 Elm st WC1
3 F 12 Elm Tree clo NW8
3 F 13 Elm Tree rd NW8
23 H 20 Elmington rd SE5
23 E 20 Elmington rd SE5
11 E 9 Elms ms W2
7 J 18 Elnathan ms W9
9 K 19 Elsham rd W14
23 G 8 Elsted st SE17

3	J 4	Elsworthy rd NW3
3	L 1	Elsworthy ri NW3
3	L 3	Elsworthy ter NW3
19	C 2	Elvaston ms SW7
19	C 2	Elvaston pl SW7
21	E 4	Elverton st SW1
8	R 12	Elwin st E2
14	U 2	Ely pl EC1
20	N 8	Elystan pl SW3
19	M 8	Elystan pl SW3
19	K 7	Elystan st SW3
6	S 5	Elystan wk N1
16	V 19	Emba st SE16
20	S 13	Embankment gdns SW3
13	L 13	Embankment pl WC2
6	O 19	Emerald st WC1
15	A 12	Emerson st SE1
21	C 3	Emery Hill st SW1
14	T 20	Emery st SE1
8	V 8	Emma st E2
19	A 4	Emperors ga SW7
18	Z 4	Emperors ga SW7
18	U 12	Empress pl SW5
23	B 13	Empress st SE17
1	L 15	Enbrook st W10
13	J 5	Endell st WC2
5	F 15	Endsleigh gdns WC1
5	F 16	Endsleigh pl WC1
5	F 15	Endsleigh st WC1
7	L 1	Enfield rd N1
12	N 1	Enford st W1
15	J 13	English Grounds SE1
24	P 1	Enid st SE16
11	K 20	Enismore gdns SW7
11	H 20	Ennismore Gdns ms SW7
19	J 1	Ennismore gdns SW7
19	J 1	Ennismore ms SW7
11	K 20	Ennismore ms SW7
19	K 1	Ennismore st SW7
19	J 1	Ennismore ter Sw7
16	T 9	Ensign st E1
19	E 9	Ensor ms SW7
18	S 17	Epirus ms SW6
18	S 17	Epirus rd SW6
7	G 17	Epworth st EC2
21	H 6	Frasmus st SW1
2	H 17	Errington rd W9
7	D 18	Errol st EC1
4	R 1	Erskine ms NW3
4	R 1	Erskine rd NW3
2	U 14	Esendine rd W9
24	T 8	Esmeralda rd SE1
2	P 5	Esmond rd NW6
14	S 7	Essex ct WC2
6	Y 4	Essex rd N1
14	R 8	Essex st WC2
10	U 19	Essex vlls W8
18	N 17	Estcourt rd SW6
21	F 6	Esterbrooke st SW1
23	B 7	Ethel st SE17
19	L 20	Ethelburga st SW11
24	V 15	Ethnard rd SE15
7	B 14	Europa pl EC1
18	T 16	Eustance rd SW6
5	E 15	Euston rd NW1
5	E 14	Euston sq NW1
5	D 14	Euston st NW1
5	D 13	Euston sta NW1
19	E 10	Evelyn gdns SW7
7	E 10	Evelyn wlk N1
13	E 4	Evelyn yd W1
6	P 5	Everilda st N1
17	H 15	Everington st W6
5	C 10	Eversholt st NW1
9	G 11	Evesham st W11
14	Z 15	Ewer st SE1
15	L 4	Exchange bldgs E1
13	L 10	Exchange ct WC2
24	N 20	Exeter rd SE15
13	M 9	Exeter st WC2
14	N 9	Exeter st WC2
9	B 10	Exhibition clo W12
19	G 2	Exhibition rd SW7
11	G 19	Exhibition rd SW7
1	H 20	Exmoor st W10
6	T 16	Exmouth mkt EC1
3	J 8	Exon st SE17
14	T 15	Exton st SE1
9	B 4	Eynham rd W10
6	S 18	Eyre St hill EC1
8	P 11	Ezra st E2

F

18	P 17	Fabian rd SW6
16	N 19	Fair st SE1
15	M 16	Fair st SE1
7	L 17	Fairchild st EC2
16	T 6	Fairclough st E1
3	C 1	Fairfax pl NW6
3	C 1	Fairfax rd NW6
3	C 2	Fairhazel gdns NW6
19	L 1	Fairhold st SW7
18	N 11	Fairholme rd W14
7	A 3	Fairstead wk N1
13	G 5	Falconberg ct W1
13	F 5	Falconberg ms W9
7	L 10	Falkirk st N1
23	B 3	Falmouth rd SE1
23	E 1	Falmouth rd SE1
18	P 12	Fane st W14
7	A 19	Fann st EC1
7	J 11	Fanshaw st N1
1	L 20	Faraday rd W10
13	E 5	Fareham st W1
18	V 16	Farm la SW6
10	S 13	Farm pl W8
12	W 11	Farm st W1
10	T 13	Farmer st W8
22	Y 19	Farmers rd SE5
16	U 18	Farncombe st SE16
18	X 9	Farnell ms SW5
14	Y 14	Farnham pl SE1
22	P 12	Farnham royal SE11
17	H 2	Faroe rd W14
6	U 10	Farringdon rd EC1
6	U 17	Farringdon rd EC1
14	W 5	Farringdon st EC4
6	U 17	Farrington la EC1
16	Y 15	Farthing fields E1
16	O 2	Fashion st E1
22	X 11	Faunce st SE17
19	A 14	Fawcett st SW10
7	E 16	Featherstone st EC1
16	T 3	Feildgate st E1
8	X 9	Felix st E2
8	Y 18	Fellbrigg st E1
7	G 5	Felton st N1
15	K 7	Fen ct EC3
15	J 7	Fenchurch av Ec3
15	L 7	Fenchurch bldgs EC3
15	J 8	Fenchurch st EC3
15	M 8	Fenchurch st sta EC3
23	L 2	Fendall st SE1
15	R 6	Fenelon pl W14
22	R 18	Fentiman rd SW8
2	P 18	Fermoy rd W9
2	P 11	Fernhead rd W9
6	S 13	Fernsbury st WC1
19	B 16	Fernshaw rd SW10
14	T 4	Fetter la EC4
14	R 1	Field ct WC1
6	U 10	Field pl EC1
17	L 13	Field rd W6
6	N 11	Field st WC1
9	H 20	Fielding rd W14
23	B 13	Fielding st SE17
6	O 7	Fife ter N1
1	K 15	Fifth av W10
18	N 19	Filmer rd SW6
18	X 12	Finborough rd SW10
3	E 8	Finchley pl NW8
3	F 3	Finchley rd NW8
14	P 19	Finck st SE1
8	X 15	Finnis st E2
15	H 1	Finsbury av EC2
15	G 2	Finsbury cir EC2
7	J 19	Finsbury mkt EC2
7	F 20	Finsbury pav EC2
7	G 20	Finsbury sq EC2
7	E 20	Finsbury st EC2
9	F 4	Finstock rd W10
2	N 16	First av W10
19	M 4	First st SW3
13	M 2	Fisher st WC1
3	F 17	Fisherton st NW8
22	S 5	Fitzalan st SE11
17	L 7	Fitzgeorge av W14
12	T 4	Fitzhardinge st W1
17	M 6	Fitzjames av W14
12	X 12	Fitzmaurice pl W1
5	B 18	Fitzroy ct W1
5	A 19	Fitzroy ms W1
4	T 2	Fitzroy rd NW1
5	A 18	Fitzroy sq W1
5	B 19	Fitzroy st W1
22	W 4	Fives ct SE11
16	R 9	Flank st E1
13	E 6	Flaxman ct W1
5	H 14	Flaxman ter WC1
14	X 5	Fleet la EC4
14	T 6	Fleet st EC4
8	S 18	Fleet St hill E1
22	X 13	Fleming rd SE17
16	T 8	Fletcher st E1
7	M 19	Fleur de Lis st E1
23	G 8	Flint st SE17
23	K 9	Flinton st SE17
13	H 5	Flitcroft st WC2
16	S 19	Flockton st SE16
19	L 11	Flood st SW3
19	K 12	Flood wlk SW3
13	L 7	Floral st WC2
6	X 2	Florence st N1
8	T 13	Florida st E2
24	V 10	Folair way SE16
13	B 1	Foley st W1
7	M 20	Folgate st E1
7	L 20	Folgate st E1
16	T 8	Forbes st E1
16	Y 3	Ford sq E1
16	V 3	Fordham st E1
2	R 14	Fordingley rd W9
15	D 2	Fore st EC2
17	D 7	Foreman ct W6
2	Z 18	Formosa st W9
3	A 18	Formosa st W9
12	N 5	Forset st W1
7	C 8	Forston st N1
22	X 14	Forsyth gdns SE17
24	R 7	Fort rd SE1
15	L 1	Fort st E1
7	B 19	Fortune st EC1
10	Z 10	Fosbury ms W2
2	V 19	Foscote ms W9
13	B 7	Fouberts pl W1
19	G 9	Foulis ter SW7
21	H 19	Fount st SW8
14	S 8	Fountain ct EC4
16	O 1	Fournier st E1
1	L 15	Fourth av W10
6	Y 2	Fowler rd N1
6	Y 20	Fox & Knot st EC1
14	S 1	Fox ct EC1
22	V 18	Foxley rd SW9
3	H 17	Frampton st NW8
21	B 4	Francis st SW1
21	H 11	Francis wharf SW1
18	R 12	Franklin sq SW5
20	R 10	Franklins row SW3
14	T 19	Frazier st SE1
24	S 1	Frean st SE16
12	S 18	Frederic ms SW1

12 N 7	Frederick clo W2	
22 W 20	Frederick cres SW9	
6 O 13	Frederick st WC1	
7 M 2	Frederick ter E8	
6 2	Freeling st N1	
23 K 8	Freemantle SE17	
8 Z 4	Fremont st E9	
7 L 14	French pl E1	
9 F 9	Freston st W10	
14 X 7	Friar st EC4	
14 X 19	Friars pl SE1	
13 C 15	Friary ct SW1	
24 U 18	Friary rd SE15	
15 A 7	Friday st EC4	
6 W 12	Friend st EC1	
13 F 7	Frith st W1	
9 B 13	Frithville gdns W12	
7 A 7	Frome st N1	
6 Z 7	Frome st N1	
6 U 8	Fryes bldgs N1	
15 M 2	Frying Pan all E1	
16 Y 18	Fulford st SE16	
18 T 18	Fulham bdy SW6	
17 E 11	Fulham Palace rd W6	
17 H 18	Fulham Palace rd SW6	
19 G 9	Fulham rd SW3	
18 T 19	Fulham rd SW6	
7 G 11	Fullwood ms N1	
11 A 9	Fulton ms W2	
14 R 2	Fulwood pl WC1	
24 T 20	Furley rd SE15	
14 T 3	Furnival st EC4	
21 F 5	Fynes st SW1	

G

5 M 20	Gage st WC1	
6 S 4	Gainford st N1	
16 O 17	Gainsford st SE1	
13 K 2	Galen pl WC1	
8 Y 14	Gales gdns E8	
24 W 6	Galley Wall rd SE16	
1 K 15	Galton st W10	
7 C 14	Galway st EC1	
14 X 15	Gambia st SE1	
13 B 7	Ganton st W1	
12 U 1	Garbutt pl W1	
6 Y 12	Gard st EC1	
10 U 10	Garden ms W2	
3 E 11	Garden rd NW8	
22 X 2	Garden row SE1	
7 J 15	Glazebury rd W14	
15 C 9	Garlick hill EC4	
6 T 13	Garnault ms EC1	
6 U 14	Garnault pl EC1	
16 Z 10	Garner st E1	
8 U 9	Garner st E2	
24 O 17	Garnies clo SE15	
7 B 17	Garrett st EC1	
13 J 9	Garrick st WC2	
13 J 9	Garrick yd WC2	
17 K 14	Garvan clo W6	
10 W 7	Garway rd W2	
8 N 12	Gascoigne pl E2	
2 T 1	Gascony av NW6	
22 R 12	Gasholder pl SE11	
6 X 4	Gaskin st N1	
17 H 13	Gastein rd W6	
11 L 19	Gate ms SW7	
14 N 3	Gate st WC2	
3 J 17	Gateforth st NW8	
7 J 16	Gatesborough st EC2	
23 C 13	Gateway SE17	
20 W 11	Gatliff rd SW1	
23 G 6	Gavel st SE17	

21 J 2	Gayfere st SW1	
22 X 2	Gaywood st SE1	
22 W 11	Gaza st SE17	
16 O 12	Gedling pl SE1	
6 Z 16	Gee st EC1	
7 A 16	Gee st EC1	
12 V 6	Gees ct W1	
7 M 9	Geffrye museum E2	
7 M 9	Geffrye st E2	
24 W 19	Geldart rd SE15	
19 G 3	Geological museum SW7	
13 L 11	George st WC2	
15 F 15	George Inn yd SE1	
16 S 19	George row SE16	
12 T 3	George st W1	
12 V 8	George yd W1	
5 B 3	Georgiana st NW1	
8 O 12	Georgina gdns E2	
20 V 6	Gerald ms SW1	
20 U 6	Gerald rd SW1	
22 U 2	GERALDINE MARY HARMSWORTH PARK SE11	
22 V 2	Geraldine st SE1	
13 G 8	Gerrard pl W1	
6 X 8	Gerrard rd N1	
13 G 8	Gerrard st W1	
14 U 20	Gerridge st SE1	
19 D 15	Gertrude st SW10	
24 Y 17	Gervase st SE15	
18 P 9	Gibbs Green est W14	
6 V 4	Gibson sq N1	
17 K 9	Giddon rd W14	
6 N 1	Gifford st N1	
5 L 2	Gifford st N1	
13 J 2	Gilbert pl WC1	
22 V 6	Gilbert rd SE11	
12 V 7	Gilbert st W1	
12 Z 2	Gildea st W1	
20 Z 5	Gillingham ms SW1	
21 A 5	Gillingham row SW1	
21 A 5	Gillingham st SW1	
20 Z 5	Gillingham st SW1	
19 C 12	Gilston rd SW10	
14 X 3	Giltspur st EC1	
17 H 4	Girdlers rd W14	
18 R 19	Gironde rd SW6	
22 W 1	Gladstone st SE1	
24 P 12	Glangall rd SE15	
8 Y 15	Glass st E2	
14 Y 18	Glasshill st SE1	
13 C 10	Glasshouse st W1	
21 M 9	Glasshouse wlk SE11	
22 N 9	Glasshouse wlk SE11	
17 L 9	Glazebury rd W14	
19 J 13	Glebe pl SW3	
19 A 8	Gledhow gdns SW5	
17 L 11	Gledstanes rd W14	
19 F 6	Glendower pl SW7	
19 Y 18	Glenfinlas way	
2 T 4	Glengall pass SW6	
2 T 4	Glengall rd SW6	
24 P 13	Glengall ter SE15	
9 B 4	Glenroy st W12	
17 A 6	Glenthorne rd W6	
4 P 18	Glentworth st SW1	
15 D 20	Globe st SE1	
12 X 7	Globe yd W1	
4 T 2	Gloucester av NW1	
4 X 4	Gloucester cres NW1	
4 W 7	Gloucester Ga ms NW1	
4 W 7	Gloucester ga NW1	
11 C 6	Gloucester Ms w W2	
11 D 6	Gloucester ms W2	
12 P 2	Gloucester Pl ms W1	
4 O 18	Gloucester pl NW1	

12 R 2	Gloucester pl W1	
19 C 8	Gloucester rd SW7	
21 B 8	Gloucester st SW1	
11 H 7	Gloucester sw W2	
11 C 6	Gloucester ter W2	
6 U 14	Gloucester way EC1	
10 U 16	Gloucester wlk W8	
22 N 11	Glyn st SE11	
19 M 3	Glynde ms SW3	
16 N 16	Goat st SE1	
18 P 19	Goaters all SW6	
19 L 9	Godfrey st SW3	
14 Z 7	Godliman st EC4	
21 M 11	Godling st SE11	
6 S 9	Godson st N1	
2 N 19	Golborne gdns W10	
9 L 1	Golborne ms W10	
1 M 20	Golborne rd W10	
9 L 1	Golborne rd W10	
7 B 17	Golden la EC1	
13 C 9	Golden sq W1	
9 B 19	Goldhawk rd W12	
2 Y 2	Goldhurst ter NW6	
3 B 1	Goldhurst ter NW6	
16 U 7	Golding st E1	
5 E 7	Goldington cres NW1	
5 F 8	Goldington st NW1	
2 T 18	Goldney rd W9	
16 U 5	Goldney ter E1	
21 G 20	Goldsboro' rd SW8	
8 T 9	Goldsmiths row E2	
8 U 7	Goldsmiths sq E2	
13 C 1	Goodge pl W1	
13 D 1	Goodge st W1	
16 R 6	Goodman st E1	
16 O 8	Goodmans yd E1	
5 J 8	Goods way NW1	
13 J 9	Goodwins ct WC2	
6 U 11	Goose yd EC1	
7 G 6	Gopsall st N1	
10 V 17	Gordon pl W8	
5 F 17	Gordon sq WC1	
5 E 16	Gordon st WC1	
19 C 1	Gore st SW7	
2 U 8	Gorefield pl NW6	
9 J 11	Gorham pl W11	
15 L 5	Goring st EC3	
17 M 6	Gorleston st W14	
8 N 11	Gorsuch pl E2	
12 Z 1	Gosfield st W1	
13 G 5	Goslett yd WC2	
8 P 13	Gosset st E2	
6 X 14	Goswell pl EC1	
6 Y 15	Goswell rd EC1	
14 U 5	Gough sq EC4	
6 P 16	Gough st WC1	
16 O 4	Goulston st E1	
5 E 16	Gower ct WC1	
13 F 1	Gower ms WC1	
5 C 15	Gower st WC1	
5 C 16	Gower st WC1	
16 S 5	Gowers wlk E1	
15 H 8	Gracechurch st EC3	
16 T 9	Graces all E1	
5 B 18	Grafton ms W1	
5 F 13	Grafton pl NW1	
12 Z 10	Grafton st W1	
5 B 18	Grafton way W1	
6 Z 10	Graham st N1	
20 T 7	Graham ter SW1	
23 F 6	Grail row SE17	
22 N 7	Granby bldgs SE11	
8 R 15	Granby st E2	
5 A 10	Granby ter NW1	
14 X 1	Grand av EC1	
14 P 6	Grange ct WC2	
23 L 2	Grange rd SE1	
7 G 7	Grange st N1	
23 M 1	Grange the SE1	
24 N 1	Grange wlk SE1	
23 L 2	Grange wlk SE1	
24 N 2	Grange yd SE1	

2 S 1	Grangeway NW6	
6 S 8	Grant st N1	
6 Y 7	Grantbridge st N1	
12 W 15	Grantham pl W1	
2 X 14	Grantully rd W9	
12 S 7	Granville pl W1	
2 T 10	Granville rd NW6	
6 R 13	Granville sq WC1	
6 P 13	Granville st WC1	
13 J 4	Grape st WC1	
17 K 2	Gratton rd W14	
15 M 4	Gravel la E1	
14 V 18	Gray st SE1	
14 P 1	Grays Inn pl WC1	
6 O 16	Grays Inn rd WC1	
14 R 1	Grays Inn sq WC1	
13 A 5	Great Castle st W1	
12 Z 5	Great Castle st W1	
4 N 20	Great Central st NW1	
13 E 5	Great Chapel st W1	
17 G 8	Great Church la W6	
21 J 1	Great College st SW1	
12 P 6	Great Cumberland Pl W1	
12 O 6	Great Cumberland ms W1	
23 F 2	Great Dover st SE1	
7 J 15	Great Eastern st EC2	
13 H 18	Great George st SW1	
15 A 13	Great Guilford st SE1	
6 O 19	Great James st WC1	
13 B 6	Great Marlborough st W1	
15 G 15	Great Maze pond SE1	
13 H 8	Great Newport st WC2	
5 M 19	Great Ormond st WC1	
6 N 19	Great Ormond st WC1	
6 P 12	Great Percy st WC1	
21 G 2	Great Peter st SW1	
21 J 2	Great Peter st SW1	
12 Z 2	Great Portland st W1	
13 A 4	Great Portland st W1	
13 D 8	Great Pulteney st W1	
13 M 5	Great Queen st WC2	
13 J 2	Great Russell st WC1	
13 J 14	Great Scotland yd SW1	
13 G 20	Great Smith st SW1	
21 H 1	Great Smith st SW1	
15 J 5	Great St. Helens EC3	
15 A 19	Great Suffolk st SE1	
14 Y 15	Great Suffolk st SE1	
6 Y 17	Great Sutton st EC1	
13 A 2	Great Titchfield st W1	
4 Z 19	Great Titchfield st W1	
15 J 9	Great Tower st EC3	
14 O 3	Great Turnstile WC1	
17 A 9	Great West rd W6	
10 S 2	Great Western rd W11	
2 R 19	Great Western rd W9	
13 E 9	Great Windmill st W1	

16 S 2	Greatorex st E1	
13 G 7	Greek st W1	
14 X 4	Green Arbour ct EC4	
16 U 14	Green bank E1	
16 Y 14	Green bank E1	
14 X 1	Green Hills rents EC1	
24 V 15	Green Hundred rd SE15	
12 Y 16	Green pk SW1	
12 S 8	Green st SE1	
23 H 2	Green wlk SE1	
3 K 10	Greenberry st NW8	
21 D 3	Greencoat pl SW1	
21 C 4	Greencoat pl SW1	
21 D 3	Greencoat row SW1	
2 Y 1	Greencroft gdns NW6	
16 U 4	Greenfield rd E1	
4 Z 4	Greenland rd NW1	
5 A 3	Greenland rd NW1	
4 Z 4	Greenland rd NW1	
4 Z 4	Greenland st NW1	
7 A 2	Greenman st N1	
6 Z 3	Greenman st N1	
13 D 8	Greens ct W1	
4 Z 18	Greenwell st W1	
14 V 16	Greet st SE1	
10 W 18	Gregory pl W8	
3 K 17	Grendon st NW8	
9 H 9	Grenfell rd W11	
19 B 6	Grenville ms SW7	
19 A 4	Grenville pl SW7	
5 L 18	Grenville st WC1	
15 C 5	Gresham st EC2	
13 E 3	Gresse st W1	
2 W 6	Greville ms NW6	
2 Y 8	Greville pl NW6	
2 Z 8	Greville rd NW6	
14 T 1	Greville st EC1	
8 O 19	Grey Eagle st E1	
21 E 3	Greycoat pl SW1	
21 E 3	Greycoat st SW1	
1 A 12	Greyhound rd NW10	
17 J 13	Greyhound rd W6	
17 G 14	Greyhound rd W6	
14 T 4	Greystoke pl EC4	
23 L 1	Griggs pl SE1	
8 P 17	Grimsby st E2	
2 T 16	Grittledon rd W9	
12 V 20	Groom pl SW1	
20 S 5	Grosvenor cotts SW1	
12 T 18	Grosvenor Cres ms SW1	
12 T 19	Grosvenor cres SW1	
20 X 1	Grosvenor Gdns Ms north SW1	
20 X 2	Grosvenor Gdns Ms north SW1	
20 X 3	Grosvenor Gdns Ms south SW1	
20 X 2	Grosvenor gdns SW1	
22 Z 17	Grosvenor pk SE5	
23 A 16	Grosvenor pk SE5	
12 W 19	Grosvenor pl SW1	
20 Y 13	Grosvenor rd SW1	
12 V 9	Grosvenor sq W1	
23 B 15	Grosvenor ter SE17	
12 Z 16	Grosvenor ter SE17	
12 U 1	Grotto pas W1	
19 L 12	Grove cotts SW3	
3 F 14	Grove End rd NW8	
3 K 14	Grove gdns NW8	
17 B 2	Grove ms W6	
6 N 18	Guildford pl WC1	
5 K 19	Guildford st WC1	
6 O 17	Guildford st WC1	
15 C 4	Guildhall EC2	
21 A 6	Guildhouse st SW1	
23 K 5	Guinness sq SE1	

15 M 1	Gun st E1	
19 B 16	Gunter gro SW10	
18 N 8	Gunterstone rd W14	
17 L 8	Gunterstone rd W14	
16 P 3	Gunthorpe st E1	
19 J 9	Guthrie st SW3	
15 G 17	Guy st SE1	
17 M 9	Gwendwr rd W14	
18 N 8	Gwendwr rd W14	
6 P 14	Gwynne pl WC1	
21 M 10	Gye st SE11	

H

17 F 3	Haarlem rd W14	
7 G 12	Haberdasher st N1	
22 R 20	Hackford rd SW9	
8 T 9	Hackney rd E2	
8 N 2	Haggerston rd E8	
8 U 14	Hague st E2	
7 J 6	Halcombe st N1	
18 R 17	Haldane rd SW6	
15 A 2	Half Moon ct EC1	
16 O 5	Half Moon pass E1	
12 Y 14	Half Moon st W1	
6 R 6	Halfmoon cres N1	
18 T 15	Halford rd SW6	
12 S 20	Halkin ms SW1	
20 S 1	Halkin pl SW1	
12 U 19	Halkin st SW1	
3 F 19	Hall pl W2	
3 C 14	Hall rd NW8	
6 X 11	Hall st EC1	
4 Y 20	Hallam ms W1	
12 Z 1	Hallam st W1	
4 Y 19	Hallam st W1	
7 D 1	Halliford st N1	
23 H 7	Halpin pl SE17	
23 G 7	Halpin pl SE17	
20 N 6	Halsey st SW3	
1 F 13	Halstow rd NW10	
6 Y 3	Halton Cross st N1	
6 Y 2	Halton rd N1	
13 D 9	Ham yd W1	
3 E 15	Hamilton clo NW8	
3 D 11	Hamilton gdns NW8	
12 V 16	Hamilton mews W1	
12 V 16	Hamilton pl	
2 Z 9	Hamilton ter NW8	
3 B 12	Hamilton ter NW8	
17 D 7	Hammersmith bdwy W6	
17 B 10	Hammersmith Br rd W6	
17 A 11	Hammersmith br W6	
17 D 9	Hammersmith fly-over W6	
9 A 20	Hammersmith gro W6	
17 C 5	Hammersmith gro W6	
17 H 6	Hammersmith rd W6	
16 N 9	Hammett st EC3	
5 G 9	Hampden clo NW1	
12 O 6	Hampden Gurney st W1	
5 B 11	Hampstead rd NW1	
2 T 13	Hampton clo NW6	
22 Z 6	Hampton st SE17	
8 S 20	Hanbury st E1	
14 P 2	Hand ct WC1	
5 K 16	Handel st WC1	
22 S 18	Handforth rd SW9	
14 V 6	Hanging Sword all EC4	
15 F 19	Hankey pl SE1	
17 L 18	Hannell rd SW6	
3 M 13	Hanover gate NW1	
22 S 16	Hanover gdns SE11	
13 L 7	Hanover pl WC2	
1 C 3	Hanover rd NW10	
12 Y 7	Hanover sq W1	
12 Z 7	Hanover st W1	
4 N 15	Hanover Ter ms NW1	

4 N 14	Hanover ter NW1	
6 Z 8	Hanover yd N1	
12 O 20	Hans cres SW1	
20 O 2	Hans pl SW1	
20 N 1	Hans rd SW3	
20 P 2	Hans st SW1	
9 J 18	Hansard ms W14	
12 A 1	Hanson st W1	
5 A 20	Hanson rd W1	
13 F 3	Hanway pl W1	
13 F 4	Hanway st W1	
16 T 9	Harads pl E1	
11 H 2	Harbet rd W2	
11 M 2	Harcourt st W1	
19 A 12	Harcourt ter SW10	
18 Z 11	Harcourt ter SW10	
1 C 6	Hardinge rd NW10	
6 T 13	Hardwick st EC1	
15 J 17	Hardwidge st SE1	
14 S 7	Hare ct EC4	
8 X 7	Hare row E2	
7 L 9	Hare wlk N1	
3 M 17	Harewood av NW1	
4 N 20	Harewood av NW1	
12 Y 6	Harewood pl W1	
3 M 20	Harewood row NW1	
19 C 11	Harley gdns SW10	
12 W 2	Harley pl W1	
3 H 2	Harley rd NW3	
12 X 2	Harley st W1	
4 W 19	Harley st W1	
22 O 13	Harleyford rd SE11	
22 S 15	Harleyford st SE11	
22 W 12	Harmsworth st SE17	
22 R 12	Harold pl SE11	
14 V 4	Harp all EC4	
15 K 10	Harp la EC3	
15 B 20	Harper rd SE1	
23 C 1	Harper rd SE1	
6 N 20	Harpur st WC1	
8 R 4	Harriet clo E8	
12 R 20	Harriet st SW1	
12 R 19	Harriet wlk SW1	
19 A 7	Harrington gdns SW7	
19 E 6	Harrington rd SW7	
5 B 9	Harrington sq NW1	
5 A 12	Harrington st NW1	
23 G 19	Harris st SE5	
5 M 14	Harrison st WC1	
15 M 3	Harrow pl E1	
1 D 14	Harrow rd NW10	
11 B 2	Harrow rd W2	
2 O 17	Harrow rd W9	
12 N 4	Harrowby st W1	
11 M 4	Harrowby st W1	
15 L 8	Hart st EC3	
14 S 1	Hart yd EC1	
21 J 20	Hartington rd SW8	
18 R 17	Hartismere rd SW6	
2 O 7	Hartland rd NW6	
7 G 5	Harvey st N1	
1 H 11	Harvist rd NW6	
2 N 9	Harvist rd NW6	
18 V 19	Harwood rd SW6	
19 M 4	Hasker st SW3	
24 S 19	Hastings clo SE15	
5 J 14	Hastings st WC1	
14 U 12	Hatfields SE1	
10 X 5	Hatherley gro W2	
21 D 6	Hatherley st SW1	
14 U 1	Hatton gdn EC1	
6 T 20	Hatton gdn EC1	
3 G 19	Hatton row NW8	
3 G 18	Hatton st NW8	
6 T 19	Hatton wall EC1	
12 X 7	Haunch of Venison rd W1	
5 M 4	Havelock st N1	
20 Z 20	Havelock ter SW8	
4 Y 1	Haven st NW1	
6 Y 10	Haverstock st N1	
23 L 14	Havil st SE5	

23 J 20	Havil st SE5	
6 X 2	Hawes st N1	
17 H 15	Hawksmoor st W6	
4 Y 1	Hawley cres NW1	
3 K 1	Hawtrey rd NW3	
12 Z 11	Hay hill W1	
10 N 5	Haydens pl W11	
10 N 5	Haydens pl W11	
16 O 7	Haydon wlk EC3	
3 M 19	Hayes pl NW1	
22 X 2	Hayles st SE11	
6 X 2	Hayman st N1	
13 F 11	Haymarket SW1	
24 S 15	Haymerle rd SE15	
6 Z 20	Hayne st EC1	
14 Z 1	Hayne st EC1	
15 H 13	Hays la SE1	
12 W 11	Hays ms W1	
14 P 13	Hayward Art gallery SE1	
6 W 17	Haywards pl EC1	
1 B 12	Hazel rd NW10	
2 S 6	Hazelmere rd NW6	
1 M 17	Hazelwood cres W10	
2 N 17	Hazelwood cres W10	
17 K 2	Hazlitt ms W14	
17 K 3	Hazlitt rd W14	
12 V 19	Headford pl SW1	
7 K 18	Hearn st EC2	
23 G 8	Hearns bldgs SE17	
6 N 15	Heathcote st WC1	
17 A 2	Hebron rd W6	
18 T 19	Heckfield pl SW6	
13 B 10	Heddon st W1	
7 A 2	Hedingham clo N1	
16 U 14	Hellings st E1	
7 B 15	Helmet row EC1	
8 X 2	Helmsley pl E8	
21 H 18	Hemans st SW8	
6 P 2	Hemingford rd N1	
8 U 17	Hemming st E1	
23 F 6	Hemp wlk SE17	
7 J 7	Hemsworth st N1	
19 L 10	Hemus pl SW3	
3 F 16	Henderson dri NW8	
23 K 7	Hendre rd SE1	
15 L 5	Heneage la EC3	
16 P 1	Heneage st E1	
19 E 13	Heniker ms SW3	
1 D 3	Henley rd NW10	
19 E 13	Henniker ms SW3	
12 W 5	Henrietta pl W1	
13 K 9	Henrietta st WC2	
18 T 6	Henriques st E1	
23 E 5	Henshaw st SE17	
3 J 7	Henstridge pl NW8	
19 L 20	Henty clo SW11	
8 Y 15	Herald st E2	
6 T 18	Herbal hill EC1	
6 U 18	Herbal pl EC1	
20 O 1	Herbert cres SW1	
1 A 8	Herbert gdns NW10	
5 J 17	Herbrand st WC1	
22 R 1	Hercules rd SE1	
10 V 6	Hereford ms W2	
10 V 5	Hereford rd W2	
19 C 7	Hereford sq SW7	
8 T 15	Hereford st E2	
6 R 9	Hermes st N1	
2 W 5	Hermit pl NW6	
6 W 12	Hermit st EC1	
11 F 2	Hermitage st W2	
16 T 14	Hermitage wall E1	
21 H 7	Herrick st SW1	
1 M 11	Herries st W10	
23 L 14	Herring st SE5	
5 B 19	Hertford pl W1	
12 V 14	Hertford st W1	
9 J 10	Hesketh pl W11	
18 Y 8	Hesper ms SW5	
16 V 5	Hessel st E1	
19 K 18	Hester rd SW11	
1 H 20	Hewer st W10	

7 K 17	Hewett st EC2	
21 M 17	Heyford av SW8	
21 L 17	Heyford ter SW8	
23 A 6	Heygate st SE17	
21 E 6	Hide pl SW1	
13 K 4	High Holborn WC1	
14 P 2	High Holborn WC1	
9 C 1	Highlever rd W10	
16 W 10	Highway the E1	
18 X 18	Hilary clo SW6	
18 U 14	Hildyard rd SW6	
1 B 11	Hiley rd NW10	
3 D 2	Hilgrove rd NW6	
1 E 20	Hill Farm rd W10	
9 E 1	Hill Farm rd W10	
3 D 10	Hill rd NW8	
12 V 12	Hill st W1	
24 Z 16	Hillbeck clo SE15	
8 O 3	Hillborough ct E8	
23 F 6	Hillery clo SE17	
10 T 13	Hillgate pl W8	
10 T 13	Hillgate st W8	
16 Z 13	Hilliards ct E1	
23 A 14	Hillingdon st SE17	
22 X 16	Hillingdon st SE5	
13 B 6	Hills pl W1	
2 Y 9	Hillside clo NW6	
10 R 13	Hillsleigh rd W8	
14 U 5	Hind ct EC4	
12 V 4	Hinde ms W1	
12 U 4	Hinde st W1	
16 U 8	Hindmarsh clo E1	
9 L 11	Hippodrome ms W11	
9 L 11	Hippodrome pl W11	
20 W 2	Hobart pl SW1	
8 R 20	Hobsons pl E1	
8 N 14	Hocker st E2	
17 J 1	Hofland rd W14	
15 K 7	Hogarth ct EC3	
18 W 7	Hogarth rd SW5	
24 U 19	Holbeck row SE15	
20 S 8	Holbein ms SW1	
20 S 9	Holbein pl SW1	
14 S 2	Holborn bldgs EC4	
14 T 2	Holborn EC1	
14 U 3	Holborn viaduct EC1	
6 P 12	Holford pl WC1	
6 R 11	Holford st WC1	
17 L 1	Holland gdns W14	
22 V 19	Holland gro SW9	
10 O 14	Holland Pk av W11	
9 J 16	Holland Pk av W11	
9 L 16	Holland Pk gdns W14	
10 N 15	Holland Pk ms W11	
18 P 2	Holland Pk rd W14	
9 M 15	Holland pk W11	
10 N 15	Holland pk W11	
18 P 17	Holland pk W8	
10 W 17	Holland pl W8	
9 K 19	Holland rd W14	
18 N 2	Holland rd W14	
10 U 18	Holland rd W14	
9 L 19	Holland Vlls rd W14	
10 R 16	Holland wlk W8	
13 D 5	Hollen st W1	
12 Y 5	Holles st W1	
19 D 11	Holly ms SW7	
8 O 1	Holly st E8	
8 Y 12	Hollybush gdns E2	
19 B 13	Hollywood ms SW10	
19 B 13	Hollywood rd SW10	
18 Z 19	Holmead rd SW6	
19 C 13	Holmes pl SW10	
14 T 17	Holmes ter SE1	
8 S 8	Holms st E2	
6 R 18	Holsworthy sq WC1	
22 W 6	Holyoak rd SE11	
17 E 18	Holyport rd SW6	
15 J 16	Holyrood st SE1	
7 L 17	Holywell la EC2	

7 J 18	Holywell row EC2	
7 K 10	Homefield st N1	
11 M 2	Homer row W1	
11 M 2	Homer st W1	
18 P 19	Homestead rd SW6	
7 A 17	Honduras st EC1	
2 P 7	Honiton rd NW6	
16 S 7	Hooper st E1	
13 J 10	Hop gdns WC2	
16 U 5	Hope Walk gdns E1	
1 M 7	Hopefield av NW6	
23 F 19	Hopewell st SE5	
9 C 15	Hopgood st W12	
13 D 7	Hopkins st W1	
14 X 12	Hopton st SE1	
23 G 13	Hopwood rd SE17	
8 P 10	Horatio st E2	
10 S 11	Horbury cres W11	
10 R 11	Horbury ms W11	
19 D 15	Horbury st SW10	
2 P 19	Hormead rd W9	
10 V 19	Hornton pl W8	
10 V 17	Hornton st W8	
13 F 8	Horse & Dolphin yd W1	
13 K 15	Horse Guards av SW1	
13 H 15	Horse Guards par SW1	
13 H 16	Horse Guards rd SW1	
15 C 12	Horse Shoe all SE1	
12 X 7	Horse Shoe yd W1	
6 X 4	Horse yd N1	
21 F 4	Horseferry rd SW1	
16 N 16	Horselydown la SE1	
23 D 13	Horsley st SE17	
23 B 16	Horsman st SE5	
19 A 17	Hortensia rd SW10	
14 X 2	Hosier la EC1	
22 S 9	Hotspur st SE11	
14 O 6	Houghton st WC2	
15 L 4	Houndsditch EC3	
13 K 20	Houses of Parliament SW1	
21 C 2	Howick pl SW1	
19 K 19	Howie pl SW11	
5 C 20	Howland Ms east W1	
5 B 20	Howland st W1	
3 D 20	Howley pl W2	
8 N 7	Hows st E2	
7 J 13	Hoxton sq N1	
7 J 7	Hoxton st N1	
24 V 17	Hoyland clo SE15	
20 Z 5	Hudsons pl SW1	
20 Y 7	Hugh ms SW1	
21 F 5	Hugh pl SW1	
20 Y 6	Hugh st SW1	
7 A 13	Hull st EC1	
7 E 2	Hullbridge ms N1	
17 L 15	Humbolt rd W6	
24 N 9	Humphrey st SE1	
14 N 13	Hungerford Foot br SE1	
9 G 12	Hunt st W11	
23 G 3	Hunter clo SE1	
5 K 16	Hunter st WC1	
6 O 1	Huntingdon st N1	
5 D 18	Huntley st WC1	
5 R 19	Hunton st E1	
13 H 10	Hunts ct WC2	
23 H 8	Huntsman st SE17	
4 O 18	Huntsworth ms NW1	
14 V 7	Hutton st EC4	
1 K 14	Huxley st W10	
12 V 17	Hyde Park Corner W1	
11 K 6	Hyde Park cres W2	
11 C 20	Hyde Park Ga ms SW7	
11 C 19	Hyde Park ga SW7	
11 J 8	Hyde Park Gdns ms W2	
11 J 9	Hyde Park gdns W2	
11 K 7	Hyde Park Sq ms W2	
11 K 7	Hyde Park sq W2	
11 K 7	Hyde Park st W2	
12 O 14	Hyde Park W2	
11 K 12	Hyde Park W2	
7 G 5	Hyde rd N1	
24 W 14	Hyndman st SE15	

I

15 J 10	Idol la EC3	
17 A 5	Iffley rd W6	
19 A 15	Ifield rd SW10	
18 Y 13	Ifield rd SW10	
1 H 13	Ilbert st W10	
10 X 9	Ilchester gdns W2	
10 P 20	Ilchester pl W14	
24 Y 9	Ilderton rd SE16	
22 Y 8	Iliffe st SE17	
22 Z 8	Iliffe St yd SE17	
7 E 6	Imber st N1	
19 E 2	Imperial Institute rd SW7	
22 U 3	Imperial War Museum SE11	
16 N 7	India st EC3	
13 D 7	Ingestre pl W1	
6 S 12	Inglebert st EC1	
16 Y 13	Inglefield sq E1	
13 K 9	Inigo pl WC2	
4 S 13	Inner crcl NW1	
14 T 7	Inner Temple la EC4	
6 S 13	Insurance st WC1	
10 W 15	Inverness gdns W8	
10 Z 8	Inverness ms W2	
10 Z 9	Inverness pl W2	
4 X 3	Inverness st NW1	
10 Z 9	Inverness ter W2	
23 G 12	Inville rd SE17	
7 A 4	Inworth wlk N1	
14 Y 8	Ireland yd EC4	
7 C 15	Ironmonger row EC1	
17 H 1	Irving rd W14	
13 H 10	Irving st WC2	
1 A 6	Irwin gdns NW10	
14 V 15	Isabella st SE1	
6 W 5	Islington grn N1	
6 V 9	Islington High st N1	
18 R 11	Ivatt pl SW6	
10 V 20	Iverna ct W8	
18 V 1	Iverna gdns W8	
19 L 6	Ives st SW3	
8 U 13	Ivimey st E2	
4 O 17	Ivor pl NW1	
7 J 8	Ivy st N1	
13 M 10	Ivybridge la WC2	
8 U 2	Ivydene rd E8	
19 K 9	Ixworth pl SW3	

J

8 V 5	Jackman st E8	
16 R 17	Jacob st SE1	
12 U 3	Jacobs Well ms W1	
16 P 19	Jamaica rd SE1	
16 X 20	Jamaica rd SE16	
12 V 6	James st W1	
13 K 8	James st WC2	
10 U 13	Jameson st W8	
4 X 2	Jamestown rd NW1	
16 U 19	Janeway st SE16	
23 K 13	Jardin st SE5	
12 V 4	Jason ct W1	
11 D 19	Jay ms SW7	
18 U 18	Jerdan pl SW6	

13 B 12	Jermyn st SW1	
3 J 15	Jerome cres NW8	
8 N 19	Jerome st E1	
8 X 13	Jersey st E2	
6 W 18	Jerusalem pass EC1	
15 M 7	Jewry st EC3	
14 V 15	Joan st SE1	
14 P 1	Jockeys fields WC1	
14 S 18	Johanna st SE1	
13 L 11	John Adam st WC2	
14 V 8	John Carpenter st EC4	
16 S 19	John Felton rd SE16	
16 R 10	John Fisher st E1	
21 G 8	John Islip st SW1	
12 Z 5	John Princes st W1	
16 Y 11	John Rennie wk E1	
24 U 1	John Roll way SE16	
23 B 14	John Ruskin st SE5	
22 Y 17	John Ruskin st SE5	
6 P 19	John st WC1	
6 O 18	Johns ms WC1	
16 Y 4	Johns pl E1	
8 T 3	Johnson clo E8	
14 U 6	Johnsons ct EC4	
21 B 12	Johnsons pl SW1	
15 G 14	Joiner st SE1	
22 O 8	Jonathan st SE11	
12 X 10	Jones st W1	
24 W 11	Joram way SE16	
24 W 11	Joram way SE16	
24 P 19	Jowett st SE15	
19 M 10	Jubilee pl SW3	
5 J 14	Judd st WC1	
19 L 19	Juer st SW11	
11 K 4	Junction ms W2	
11 H 4	Junction pl W2	
19 J 15	Justice wlk SW3	
22 P 5	Juxon st SE11	

K

8 T 9	Kay st E2	
14 N 6	Kean st WC2	
14 N 5	Keeley st WC2	
24 V 1	Keetons rd SE16	
9 E 4	Kelfield gdns W10	
14 V 20	Kell st SE1	
8 V 15	Kelsey st E2	
18 Y 2	Kelso pl W8	
18 P 20	Kelvedon rd SW6	
14 N 8	Kemble st WC2	
1 G 10	Kempe rd NW6	
18 V 11	Kempsford gdns SW5	
22 U 7	Kempsford rd SE11	
18 W 20	Kempson rd SW6	
21 K 20	Kenchester clo SW8	
11 M 6	Kendal st W2	
12 S 3	Kendall pl W1	
19 F 6	Kendrick ms SW7	
19 F 6	Kendrick pl SW7	
2 R 3	Kenilworth rd NW6	
9 K 12	Kenley wlk W11	
2 P 17	Kennet rd W9	
22 V 10	Kennings way SE11	
22 O 12	Kennington gro SE11	
22 V 8	Kennington la SE11	
22 P 15	Kennington oval SE11	
22 W 14	Kennington Pk gdns SE11	
22 V 13	Kennington Pk pl SE11	
22 V 11	Kennington Pk rd SE11	
22 U 15	Kennington pk SE11	
22 T 11	Kennington rd SE11	
12 S 1	Kenrick pl W1	
2 N 17	Kensal rd W10	

1	J 16	Kensal rd W10
10	W 18	Kensington Ch ct W8
10	V 14	Kensington Ch st W8
10	W 18	Kensington Ch wlk W8
10	Z 20	Kensington Ct pl W8
10	Z 19	Kensington ct W8
11	B 20	Kensington ga W8
10	X 7	Kensington Gdns Sq W2
11	F 19	Kensington gore SW7
18	R 2	Kensington High st W8
10	W 19	Kensington High st W8
10	V 13	Kensington mall W8
10	W 12	Kensington Pal gdns W8
10	Y 15	Kensington Palace London museum W8
10	P 10	Kensington Pk gdns W11
10	N 6	Kensington Pk ms W11
10	O 7	Kensington Pk rd W11
10	T 14	Kensington pl W8
11	D 19	Kensington rd SW7
10	X 20	Kensington sq W8
4	N 15	Kent pas NW1
8	P 7	Kent st E2
3	M 14	Kent ter NW1
11	L 19	Kent yd SW7
15	E 16	Kentish bldgs SE1
4	Z 2	Kentish Town rd NW1
5	K 16	Kenton st WC1
18	W 7	Kenway rd SW5
17	G 20	Kenyon st SW6
15	A 15	Keppel row SE1
5	G 20	Keppel st WC1
1	G 9	Keslake rd NW6
14	Y 20	Key North st SE1
24	O 4	Keyse rd SE1
5	M 10	Keystone cres N1
22	Y 1	Keyworth st SE1
22	O 19	Kibworth st SW8
2	T 3	Kilburn High rd NW6
1	K 11	Kilburn la W10
2	O 10	Kilburn la W9
2	V 12	Kilburn Pk rd NW6
2	V 5	Kilburn pl NW6
2	X 7	Kilburn priory NW6
2	T 5	Kilburn sq NW6
2	W 5	Kilburn vale est NW6
10	V 5	Kildare gdns W2
10	V 4	Kildare ter W2
6	N 10	Killick st N1
17	M 20	Kilmaine rd SW6
17	A 5	Kilmarsh rd W6
1	L 13	Kilravock st W10
1	M 3	Kimberley rd NW6
24	V 20	Kincaid rd SE15
16	W 6	Kinder st E1
23	C 9	King and Queen st SE17
13	J 17	King Charles st SW1
8	Y 3	King Edwards rd E9
14	Z 4	King Edwards st EC1
22	T 1	King Edwards wlk SE1
4	P 2	King Georges ms NW1

4	P 2	King Georges ter NW1
3	K 1	King Henrys rd NW3
4	O 1	King Henrys rd NW3
14	Y 19	King James st SE1
7	L 16	King John ct EC2
6	Z 13	King sq EC1
15	C 5	King st EC2
13	C 14	King st SW1
17	B 7	King st W6
13	K 9	King st WC2
15	F 7	King William st EC4
14	Z 2	Kinghorn st EC1
23	J 11	Kinglake st SE17
23	L 9	Kinglake st SE17
13	B 8	Kingly ct W1
13	B 7	Kingly st W1
14	Y 17	Kings Bench st SE1
14	T 8	Kings Bench wlk EC4
5	K 9	Kings Cross station N1
6	O 12	Kings Cross rd WC1
24	Y 20	Kings gro SE15
15	F 15	Kings Head yd SE1
15	B 20	Kings pl SE1
6	P 19	Kings pl WC1
20	T 4	Kings rd SW1
19	J 12	Kings rd SW3
18	Z 20	Kings rd SW6
21	B 4	Kings Scholars pas SW1
5	A 6	Kings ter NW1
9	D 3	Kingsbridge rd W10
14	W 8	Kingscote st EC4
9	H 15	Kingsdale gdns W11
9	J 7	Kingsdown clo W11
2	T 2	Kingsgate pl NW6
2	U 2	Kingsgate rd NW6
3	L 6	Kingsland NW8
7	L 6	Kingsland rd E2
18	Z 2	Kingsley ms W8
2	P 3	Kingsley rd NW6
3	G 9	Kingsmill ter NW8
4	S 4	Kingstown st NW1
13	M 4	Kingsway Hall WC2
14	N 5	Kingsway WC2
1	L 7	Kingswood av NW6
21	L 19	Kingswood clo SW8
16	T 1	Kingward st E1
17	L 20	Kingwood rd SW6
12	R 18	Kinnerton Pl north SW1
12	R 19	Kinnerton Pl south SW1
12	S 20	Kinnerton st SW1
12	S 19	Kinnerton yd SW1
17	L 14	Kinnoul rd W6
24	N 4	Kintore st SE1
15	G 18	Kipling st SE1
15	J 17	Kirby gro SE1
6	U 20	Kirby st EC1
14	U 1	Kirby st EC1
13	E 1	Kirkman pl W1
21	B 17	Kirtling st SW8
8	P 13	Kirton gdns E2
22	Z 18	Kirwin way SE5
23	D 17	Kitson rd SE5
18	X 6	Knaresborough pl SW5
14	Z 8	Knightrider st EC4
22	W 7	Knights wlk SE11
12	N 19	Knightsbridge grn SW7
11	L 18	Knightsbridge SW7
12	O 18	Knightsbridge SW7
18	T 15	Knivett rd SW6
12	O 1	Knox st W1
18	V 11	Kramer mews SW5
19	A 2	Kynance mans SW7
19	A 2	Kynance ms SW7
19	A 1	Kynance pl SW7

L

24	Z 20	Laburnum clo SE15
7	M 6	Laburnum st E2
8	N 6	Laburnum st E2
7	G 20	Lackington st EC2
9	L 6	Ladbroke cres W11
10	O 9	Ladbroke gdns W11
1	H 15	Ladbroke gro W10
9	K 3	Ladbroke gro W10
10	P 13	Ladbroke gro W11
10	O 13	Ladbroke rd W11
10	P 10	Ladbroke Sq gdns W11
10	R 11	Ladbroke sq W11
10	R 12	Ladbroke ter W11
10	R 12	Ladbroke wlk W11
16	N 17	Lafone st SE1
17	F 1	Lakeside rd W14
9	G 20	Lakeside rd W14
8	X 1	Lamb la E8
8	N 20	Lamb st E1
7	M 20	Lamb st E1
15	J 19	Lamb wlk SE1
6	R 2	Lambert st N1
21	L 4	Lambeth br SW1
22	N 5	Lambeth High st SE1
22	O 7	Lambeth ms SE11
14	O 20	Lambeth Palace rd SE1
22	N 2	Lambeth Palace rd SE1
22	O 3	Lambeth palace SE1
21	M 3	Lambeth Pier SW1
22	P 3	Lambeth rd SE1
16	S 6	Lambeth st E1
22	O 7	Lambeth wlk SE11
7	D 18	Lambs bldgs EC1
14	N 1	Lambs Conduit pas WC1
6	N 19	Lambs Conduit st WC1
7	D 19	Lambs pas EC1
10	S 8	Lambton pl W11
22	X 4	Lamlash st SE11
19	E 15	Lamont Rd pas SW10
19	E 15	Lamont rd SW10
17	K 15	Lampeter sq W6
17	F 15	Lanarch rd W6
3	D 17	Lanark pl W9
3	B 14	Lanark rd W9
2	Z 12	Lanark rd W9
12	Y 8	Lancashire ct W1
18	S 20	Lancaster ct SW6
11	C 10	Lancaster ga W2
11	D 9	Lancaster ms W2
14	N 9	Lancaster pl WC2
10	O 4	Lancaster rd W11
9	L 5	Lancaster rd W11
11	F 8	Lancaster ter W2
2	O 14	Lancefield st W10
12	N 19	Lancelot pl SW7
14	S 18	Lancelot st SE1
5	F 13	Lancing st NW1
20	O 1	Landon pl SW3
14	T 20	Lanfranc st SE1
18	O 11	Lanfrey pl W14
16	V 7	Langdale st E1
3	D 9	Langford clo NW8
3	D 9	Langford pl NW8
12	Z 3	Langham pl W1
12	Z 2	Langham st W1
1	E 11	Langler rd NW10
13	K 7	Langley ct WC2
21	M 14	Langley la SW8
13	K 7	Langley st WC2
17	G 20	Langthorne st SW6
6	O 15	Langton clo WC1
22	Y 20	Langton rd SW9
19	D 16	Langton st SW10
2	Y 5	Langtry rd NW8
2	U 16	Lanhill rd W9

10 N 10 Lansdowne cres W11
8 V 3 Lansdowne dri E8
21 K 20 Lansdowne gdns SW8
10 N 14 Lansdowne ms W11
23 G 1 Lansdowne pl SE1
10 N 12 Lansdowne rd W11
9 M 9 Lansdowne rd W11
9 M 10 Lansdowne ri W11
12 Y 12 Lansdowne row W1
5 M 17 Lansdowne ter WC1
10 O 12 Lansdowne wlk W11
15 A 18 Lant st SE1
23 C 7 Larcom st SE17
8 Z 6 Lark row E2
9 C 4 Latimer pl W10
9 D 5 Latimer rd W10
24 R 15 Latona rd SE15
22 N 10 Laud st SE11
2 X 15 Lauderdale rd W9
3 A 15 Lauderdale rd W9
19 A 2 Launceston pl W8
17 K 15 Laundry rd W6
18 Y 8 Laverton ms SW5
18 Y 7 Laverton pl SW5
14 Z 14 Lavington st SE1
5 M 8 Lavinia gro N1
23 G 1 Law st SE1
5 B 2 Lawfords wharf NW1
22 N 15 Lawn la SW8
21 M 14 Lawn la SW8
5 L 4 Lawrence pl N1
19 J 15 Lawrence st SW3
22 Y 18 Laxley clo SE5
4 Z 16 Laxton pl NW1
24 X 4 Layard sq SE16
6 S 18 Laystall st EC1
6 U 7 Layton rd N1
15 J 6 Leadenhall market
          EC3
15 J 7 Leadenhall pl EC3
15 K 6 Leadenhall st EC3
14 R 18 Leake st SE1
10 R 3 Leamington Rd vlls
          W11
17 A 7 Leamore st W6
14 T 2 Leather la EC1
6 T 19 Leather lo EC1
15 H 18 Leathermarket st
          SE1
19 F 10 Lecky st SW7
10 T 7 Ledbury Ms north
          W11
10 S 8 Ledbury Ms west
          W11
10 S 7 Ledbury rd W11
24 U 17 Ledbury st SE15
7 M 3 Lee st E8
8 N 3 Lee st E8
6 N 12 Leeke st WC1
12 T 8 Lees pl W1
13 G 9 Leicester ct WC2
13 G 9 Leicester pl WC2
13 G 10 Leicester sq WC2
13 F 9 Leicester st WC2
1 C 9 Leigh gdns NW10
15 A 17 Leigh Hunt st SE1
14 T 1 Leigh pl EC1
5 J 15 Leigh st WC1
1 C 7 Leighton gdns NW10
11 B 7 Leinster gdns W2
11 B 10 Leinster ms W2
11 A 7 Leinster pl W2
2 T 12 Leinster rd NW6
10 W 7 Leinster sq W2
11 B 10 Leinster ter W2
2 U 4 Leith yd NW6
8 S 5 Lelitia clo E8
16 R 17 Leman st E1
17 D 2 Lena gdns W6
20 N 4 Lennox Gdns ms SW1
20 N 4 Lennox gdns SW1
19 B 5 Lenthall pl SW7
24 U 10 Lenville way SE16

24 Z 17 Leo st SE15
6 Y 18 Leo yd EC1
7 F 16 Leonard st EC2
24 T 19 Leontine clo SE15
22 N 10 Leopold wlk SE11
23 J 3 Leroy st SE1
18 N 19 Letterstone rd SW6
7 A 14 Lever st EC1
6 Y 14 Lever st EC1
19 M 6 Leverett st SW3
13 G 19 Lewisham st SW1
18 Y 4 Lexham Gdns ms W8
18 X 4 Lexham gdns W8
18 V 4 Lexham ms W8
18 Y 3 Lexham wlk W8
13 D 8 Lexington st W1
15 M 3 Leyden st E1
16 N 3 Leyden st E1
14 X 19 Library st SE1
1 C 7 Liddell gdns NW10
5 B 10 Lidlington pl NW1
3 K 17 Lilestone st NW8
18 V 13 Lillie Bridge ms
          SW6
17 H 16 Lillie rd SW6
18 P 14 Lillie rd SW6
18 U 13 Lillie rd SW6
21 D 8 Lillington Gdn est
          SW1
17 J 8 Lily clo W14
10 V 11 Lime ct W8
9 B 16 Lime gro W12
15 J 7 Lime st EC3
19 D 14 Limestone st SW10
24 T 18 Limpston Gdn est
          SE15
2 N 3 Lincoln ms NW6
20 O 8 Lincoln st SW3
14 O 5 Lincolns Inn
          fields WC2
1 E 11 Linden av NW10
10 V 11 Linden gdns W2
10 U 11 Linden ms W2
16 Z 1 Lindley st E1
14 Y 1 Lindsey st EC1
4 N 18 Linhope st NW1
24 S 5 Linsey st SE16
7 C 5 Linton st N1
1 K 20 Lionel ms W10
18 N 6 Lisgar ter W14
13 G 9 Lisle st WC2
3 G 15 Lisson gro NW8
3 K 20 Lisson st NW1
22 X 20 Listowell clo SW9
22 X 20 Listowell st SW9
13 H 8 Litchfield st WC2
24 Y 5 Litlington st SE16
4 Z 14 Little Albany st
          NW1
13 A 6 Little Argyll st
          W1
18 Z 10 Little Boltons the
          SW5
19 A 11 Little Boltons the
          SW10
15 A 3 Little Britain EC1
14 Y 2 Little Britain EC1
12 W 20 Little Chester st
          SW1
21 J 2 Little College st
          SW1
15 C 16 Little Dorrit ct
          SE1
14 R 8 Little Essex st
          WC2
14 R 8 Little Essex st
          WC2
13 J 19 Little George st
          SW1
13 B 7 Little Marlborough
          st W1
14 V 5 Little New st EC4
13 G 9 Little Newport st WC2

13 A 4 Little Portland st
          W1
13 J 2 Little Russell st
          WC1
13 H 19 Little Sanctuary
          SW1
21 H 2 Little Smith st
          SW1
16 N 6 Little Somerset st
          E1
13 B 15 Little St. James
          st SW1
13 A 3 Little Titchfield
          st W1
14 N 3 Little Turnstile
          WC1
23 C 11 Liverpool gro SE17
6 U 2 Liverpool rd N1
15 K 2 Liverpool St
          station EC2
15 J 2 Liverpool st EC2
24 T 14 Livesey pl SE15
13 D 7 Livonia st W1
7 C 15 Lizard st EC1
16 T 18 Llewellyn st SE16
6 S 12 Lloyd Baker st WC1
6 R 13 Lloyd sq WC1
6 S 12 Lloyd st WC1
15 L 7 Lloyds av EC3
6 V 13 Lloyds row EC1
17 E 13 Lochaline st W6
24 W 2 Lockwood sq SE16
15 F 18 Lockyer st SE1
3 H 15 Lodge rd NW8
16 U 18 Loftie st SE16
6 S 1 Lofting rd N1
18 T 5 Logan ms W8
18 T 5 Logan pl W8
22 S 7 Lollard st SE11
14 Y 16 Loman st SE11
8 U 19 Lomas st S1
14 U 7 Lombard la EC4
15 G 7 Lombard st EC3
10 Y 10 Lombardy pl W2
23 D 19 Lomond gro SE5
23 L 13 Loncroft rd SE5
15 F 12 London br EC4
15 F 14 London Br st SE1
15 H 14 London Bridge
          station SE1
8 W 2 London Fields East
          side E8
11 G 5 London ms W2
22 X 2 London rd SE1
15 K 8 London st EC3
11 G 6 London st W2
15 G 3 London wall EC2
13 L 6 Long acre WC2
14 Y 1 Long la EC1
15 D 18 Long la SE1
11 M 1 Long st E2
23 L 1 Long wlk SE1
6 N 18 Long yd WC1
4 Z 16 Longford st NW1
24 S 10 Longland ct SE1
24 S 6 Longley st SE1
21 B 7 Longmore st SW1
18 T 7 Longridge rd SW5
13 G 11 Longs ct WC2
22 X 5 Longville rd SE11
6 U 2 Lonsdale pl N1
2 O 6 Lonsdale rd NW6
10 R 7 Lonsdale rd W11
6 T 2 Lonsdale sq N1
2 Y 20 Lord Hills rd W2
21 J 2 Lord North st SW1
18 X 19 Lord Roberts ms
          SW6
8 P 13 Lorden wlk E2
3 G 13 Lords Cricket grd
          NW8
19 K 15 Lordship pl SW3
6 O 11 Lorenzo st WC1

17 D 2 Loris rd W6
3 L 15 Lorne clo NW8
9 J 17 Lorne gdns W11
22 Y 14 Lorrimore rd SE17
22 Z 13 Lorrimore sq SE17
24 U 10 Losbeine way SE16
15 F 5 Lothbury EC2
22 Y 20 Lothian ms SW9
22 Y 20 Lothian rd SW9
1 L 13 Lothrop st W10
19 A 19 Lots rd SW10
3 D 5 Loudon rd NW8
22 R 10 Loughborough st SE11
15 H 10 Lovat la EC3
24 T 12 Lovegrove st SE1
8 O 2 Lovermere rd E8
20 W 2 Lower Belgrave st SW1
20 Y 1 Lower Grosvenor pl SW1
13 C 9 Lower James st W1
13 C 9 Lower John st W1
17 B 11 Lower Mall W6
14 R 19 Lower Marsh SE1
3 K 1 Lower Merton ri NW3
20 R 8 Lower Sloane st SW1
15 G 10 Lower Thames st EC3
20 U 2 Lowndes clo SW1
13 B 7 Lowndes ct W1
20 T 2 Lowndes pl SW1
12 R 19 Lowndes sq SW1
20 S 1 Lowndes st SW1
16 Y 9 Lowood st E1
5 L 13 Loxham st WC1
19 K 6 Lucan pl SW3
10 V 13 Lucerne ms W8
24 T 4 Lucey rd SE16
14 X 7 Ludgate broadway EC4
14 W 6 Ludgate cir EC4
14 X 6 Ludgate hill EC4
14 Y 7 Ludgate sq EC4
7 H 17 Luke st EC2
13 L 9 Lumley ct WC2
12 U 7 Lumley st W1
20 Z 11 Lupus st SW1
21 A 11 Lupus st SW1
17 H 13 Lurgan av W6
21 J 17 Luscombe way SW8
3 H 18 Luton st NW8
4 T 19 Luxborough st W1
17 E 5 Luxemburg gdns W6
20 T 2 Lyall ms SW1
20 S 3 Lyall Ms west SW1
20 S 3 Lyall st SW1
2 R 15 Lydford rd W9
23 L 17 Lydney clo SE15
20 X 3 Lygon pl SW1
5 A 2 Lyme st NW1
5 B 2 Lyme ter NW1
23 K 17 Lynbrook clo SE15
2 P 7 Lynton rd NW6
24 X 8 Lynton rd SE1
3 F 17 Lyons pl NW8
17 G 18 Lysia st SW6
23 E 12 Lytham st SE17
3 K 1 Lyttelton clo NW3

M

5 H 14 Mabeldon pl NW1
13 F 9 Macclesfield st W1
9 C 13 Macfarlane pl W12
9 C 14 Macfarlane rd W12
4 U 18 Macfarren pl NW1
3 L 9 Mackennal st NW8
13 L 4 Macklin st WC2

24 T 5 Macks rd SE16
5 A 11 Mackworth st NW1
23 B 12 Macleod st SE17
17 K 3 Maclise rd W14
2 R 12 Macroom rd W9
4 S 19 Madame Tussauds NW8
12 Y 8 Maddox st W1
13 A 7 Maddox st W1
23 L 8 Madron st SE17
16 P 8 Magdalen pas E1
15 K 18 Magdalen st SE1
22 T 14 Magee st SE11
14 U 8 Magpie all EC4
16 P 16 Maguire st SE1
3 E 19 Maida av W2
3 C 14 Maida vale W9
5 L 7 Maiden La br N1
13 L 9 Maiden la WC2
15 D 15 Maidstone bldgs SE1
8 T 8 Maidstone st E2
7 L 11 Mail Coach yd E2
24 T 16 Maisemore st SE15
16 U 20 Major rd SE16
24 U 1 Major rd SE16
19 L 7 Makins st SW3
5 E 18 Malet pl WC1
5 F 19 Malet st WC1
13 D 15 Mall the SW1
19 G 13 Mallord st SW3
3 L 17 Mallory st NW8
7 E 15 Mallow st EC1
24 S 13 Malt st SE1
6 X 15 Malta st EC1
24 N 1 Maltby st SE1
16 N 19 Maltby st SE1
9 K 4 Malton ms W10
9 J 4 Malton rd W10
14 P 8 Maltravers st WC2
10 N 1 Malvern clo W10
2 P 11 Malvern gdns W9
2 R 11 Malvern pl W9
8 S 1 Malvern rd E8
2 S 12 Malvern rd NW6
6 S 3 Malvern ter N1
3 C 11 Man in Moon pas W1
1 K 18 Manchester dri W10
12 T 3 Manchester ms W1
12 U 4 Manchester sq W1
12 T 2 Manchester st W1
15 F 20 Manciple st SE1
12 U 4 Mandeville pl W1
13 G 6 Manette st W1
4 T 3 Manley st NW1
16 R 5 Manningtree st E1
1 H 1 Manor Ho dri NW6
22 Y 10 Manor pl SE17
23 A 9 Manor rd SE17
19 J 11 Manresa rd SW3
16 O 7 Mansell st E1
12 X 2 Mansfield ms W1
12 X 2 Mansfield st W1
8 U 10 Mansford st E2
15 E 6 Mansion House st EC2
19 D 6 Manson ms SW7
19 E 7 Manson pl SW7
6 T 7 Mantell st N1
8 V 16 Mape st E2
5 B 19 Maple pl W1
5 C 19 Maple st W1
2 O 12 Marban rd W9
18 R 13 Marchbank rd SW5
5 K 17 Marchmont st WC1
23 K 20 Marchwood clo SE5
23 M 7 Marcia rd SE1
17 A 3 Marco rd W6
8 Y 2 Mare st E8
13 A 4 Margaret ct W1
12 Z 4 Margaret st W1
13 A 4 Margaret st W1
19 L 13 Margaretta ter SW3

6 R 15 Margery st WC1
17 H 10 Margravine gdns W6
17 H 12 Margravine rd W6
8 V 7 Marian pl E2
8 W 8 Marian st E2
16 V 19 Marigold st SE16
24 R 1 Marine st SE16
15 K 8 Mark la EC3
7 H 16 Mark st EC2
13 A 5 Market ct W1
12 W 14 Market ms W1
13 A 5 Market pl W1
20 N 9 Markham sq SW3
19 M 9 Markham st SW3
8 S 4 Marlborough av E8
22 Z 7 Marlborough clo SE17
13 B 7 Marlborough ct W1
24 S 12 Marlborough gro SE1
3 D 6 Marlborough hill NW8
13 D 15 Marlborough ho SW1
3 B 9 Marlborough pl NW8
13 D 15 Marlborough rd SW1
19 K 8 Marlborough rd SW3
18 W 4 Marloes rd W8
3 F 4 Marloes the NW8
24 U 20 Marmont rd SE15
1 L 12 Marne st W10
22 X 2 Marshall gdns SE1
13 C 7 Marshall st W1
15 C 17 Marshalsea rd SE1
21 H 3 Marsham st SW1
13 L 8 Mart st WC2
16 Z 7 Martha st E1
15 F 9 Martin la EC4
13 L 7 Martlett ct WC2
18 O 20 Marville rd SW6
24 U 10 Marwood way SE16
9 J 10 Mary pl W11
7 B 5 Mary st N1
4 Z 6 Mary ter NW1
7 A 3 Maryland wlk N1
2 V 18 Marylands rd W9
4 U 20 Marylebone High st W1
12 U 1 Marylebone High st W1
12 V 5 Marylebone la W1
12 V 2 Marylebone ms W1
13 B 4 Marylebone pas W1
4 V 18 Marylebone rd NW1
12 U 2 Marylebone st W1
4 N 19 Marylebone station NW1
22 R 8 Marylee way
9 H 20 Masbro rd W14
12 Z 7 Masons Arms ms W1
23 H 5 Masons st SE17
13 C 12 Masons yd SW1
23 J 6 Massinger st SE1
18 O 6 Matheson rd W14
6 O 4 Matilda st N1
13 G 19 Matthew Parker st SW1
16 R 13 Maudlins grn E1
21 E 4 Maunsel st SW1
24 P 10 Mawbey pl SE1
24 P 11 Mawbey rd SE1
21 K 20 Mawbey st SW8
18 Y 19 Maxwell rd SW6
18 N 12 May st W14
12 Z 12 Mayfair pl W1
8 N 1 Mayfield rd E8
16 Z 18 Mayflower st SE16
6 R 7 Maygood st N1
24 R 15 Maymerle rd SE15
13 J 10 Mays ct WC2
2 U 2 Mazenod av NW6
22 S 1 McAuley clo SE1
10 P 3 McGregor rd W11
18 Z 4 McLeods ms SW7

19 A 4	McLeods ms SW7	
22 T 1	Mead row SE1	
22 V 14	Meadcroft rd SE11	
22 O 16	Meadow ms SW8	
21 M 18	Meadow pl SW8	
22 O 15	Meadow rd SW8	
23 A 3	Meadow row SE1	
17 E 19	Meadowbank clo SW6	
4 O 2	Meadowbank NW3	
13 E 7	Meard st W1	
6 N 17	Mecklenburg pl WC1	
6 N 16	Mecklenburg sq WC1	
6 N 15	Mecklenburg st WC1	
5 E 8	Medburn st NW1	
6 U 10	Medcalf pl N1	
23 B 20	Medlar st SE5	
22 F 3	Medway st SW1	
16 X 13	Meeting Ho all E1	
24 W 20	Meeting Ho la SE15	
14 O 7	Melbourne pl WC2	
18 R 1	Melbury ct W8	
23 J 20	Melbury dr SE5	
18 O 1	Melbury rd W14	
3 M 19	Melbury ter NW1	
4 N 19	Melcombe pl NW1	
4 P 19	Melcombe st NW1	
3 E 14	Melina pl NW8	
15 H 16	Melior pl SE1	
15 H 16	Melior st SE1	
10 W 16	Melon pl W8	
17 D 1	Melrose gdns W6	
9 D 20	Melrose ter W6	
24 X 11	Meltham way SE16	
24 W 11	Meltham way SE16	
5 D 15	Melton st NW1	
7 A 2	Melville st N1	
7 A 17	Memel st EC1	
18 N 16	Mendora rd SW6	
14 R 16	Mepham st SE1	
13 J 68	Mercer st WC2	
8 X 18	Merceron st E1	
6 V 14	Meredith st EC1	
6 T 14	Merlin st WC1	
15 E 16	Mermaid ct SE1	
23 D 1	Merrick sq SE1	
18 U 13	Merrington rd SW6	
23 D 12	Morrow st SE17	
23 F 11	Merrow st SE17	
2 U 1	Messina av NW6	
22 U 11	Methley st SE11	
1 F 20	Methwold rd W10	
9 F 1	Methwold rd W10	
14 V 14	Meymott st SE1	
7 C 11	Micawber st N1	
18 U 15	Micklethwaite rd SW6	
1 K 17	Middle row W10	
14 Z 1	Middle st EC1	
14 S 7	Middle Temple la EC4	
3 F 3	Middlefield NW8	
14 Z 2	Middlesex pas EC1	
15 M 3	Middlesex st E1	
16 N 5	Middlesex st E1	
13 A 2	Middleton bldgs W1	
7 M 1	Middleton rd E8	
8 O 1	Middleton rd E8	
8 W 11	Middleton st E2	
5 C 18	Midford pl W1	
5 L 13	Midhope st WC1	
5 H 12	Midland rd NW1	
19 C 12	Milborne gro SW10	
14 X 19	Milcote st SE1	
3 J 20	Miles pl NW1	
21 K 15	Miles st SW8	
14 R 7	Milford la WC2	
14 S 8	Milford la WC2	
16 S 3	Milfred st E1	
7 L 5	Mill row N1	
16 P 18	Mill st SE1	
12 Z 8	Mill st W1	
21 K 7	Millbank SW1	
5 A 7	Miller st NW1	

6 N 17	Millman ms WC1	
6 N 18	Millman st WC1	
16 N 19	Millstream rd SE1	
9 J 2	Millwood st W10	
1 J 8	Milman rd NW6	
19 G 16	Milman st SW10	
6 V 3	Milner pl N1	
6 V 2	Milner sq N1	
20 N 5	Milner st SW3	
17 J 1	Milson rd W14	
7 D 20	Milton ct EC2	
7 D 20	Milton st EC2	
1 D 1	Milverton rd NW6	
22 U 11	Milverton st SE11	
16 X 1	Milward st E1	
23 M 9	Mina rd SE17	
15 K 8	Mincing la EC3	
20 U 6	Minera ms SW1	
8 W 9	Minerva st E2	
9 F 19	Minford gdns W14	
16 N 8	Minories EC3	
15 B 17	Mint st SE1	
7 G 8	Mintern st N1	
8 W 12	Minto pl E2	
18 P 17	Mirabel rd SW6	
7 B 15	Mitchell st EC1	
4 U 17	Mitre rd SE1	
5 M 6	Mitre sq EC3	
5 L 6	Mitre st EC3	
14 W 5	Modern ct EC4	
11 M 3	Molyneux st W1	
21 G 3	Monck st SW1	
11 H 20	Moncorvo clo SW7	
22 U 5	Monkton st SE11	
10 W 6	Monmouth pl W2	
10 W 7	Monmouth rd W2	
13 J 8	Monmouth st WC2	
24 T 6	Monnow rd SE1	
12 R 2	Montagu mans W1	
12 P 2	Montagu Ms north W1	
12 P 5	Montagu Ms south W1	
12 P 4	Montagu Ms west W1	
12 P 2	Montagu pl W1	
13 H 1	Montagu rd NW1	
12 R 2	Montagu row W1	
12 P 3	Montagu sq W1	
12 P 4	Montagu st W1	
15 E 13	Montague clo SE1	
5 H 20	Montague pl WC1	
13 J 1	Montague st WC1	
22 S 12	Montford pl SE11	
16 R 2	Monthope st E1	
11 M 20	Montpelier ms SW7	
11 L 20	Montpelier pl SW7	
24 X 20	Montpelier rd SE15	
11 L 20	Montpelier sq SW7	
11 M 20	Montpelier st SW7	
11 L 20	Montpelier wlk SW7	
14 O 8	Montreal pl WC2	
1 M 7	Montrose av NW6	
11 H 20	Montrose ct SW7	
12 U 19	Montrose pl SW1	
15 H 10	Monument st EC3	
6 V 4	Moon st N1	
15 D 1	Moor la EC2	
7 E 20	Moor la EC2	
15 F 2	Moor pl EC2	
13 G 7	Moor st W1	
18 V 20	Moore Pk rd SW6	
20 O 5	Moore st SW3	
15 E 2	Moorfields EC2	
15 F 2	Moorgate EC2	
10 T 5	Moorhouse rd W2	
7 C 13	Mora st EC1	
17 J 7	More clo W14	
23 C 8	Morecambe st SE17	
6 Y 12	Moreland st EC1	
21 C 9	Moreton pl SW1	
21 D 10	Moreton st SW1	
21 C 9	Moreton ter SW1	
10 N 1	Morgan rd W10	

15 J 14	Morgans la SE1	
6 U 1	Morland ms N1	
14 U 19	Morley st SE1	
18 O 8	Mornington av W14	
5 A 8	Mornington cres NW1	
4 Z 9	Mornington pl NW1	
5 A 9	Mornington pl NW1	
4 Y 8	Mornington st NW1	
4 Y 7	Mornington ter NW1	
21 B 3	Morpeth ter SW1	
16 Y 7	Morris st E1	
2 W 14	Morshead rd W9	
2 Y 6	Mortimer cres NW6	
5 D 18	Mortimer mkt WC1	
2 X 6	Mortimer pl NW6	
7 K 2	Mortimer rd N1	
1 D 12	Mortimer rd NW10	
9 H 11	Mortimer sq W11	
12 Z 3	Mortimer st W1	
13 B 3	Mortimer st W1	
18 X 7	Morton ms SW5	
22 S 2	Morton pl SE1	
7 D 2	Morton rd N1	
13 F 2	Morwell st WC1	
10 X 8	Moscow pl W2	
10 W 9	Moscow rd W2	
24 Z 6	Mossington rd SE16	
19 L 6	Mossop st SW3	
1 F 11	Mostyn gdns NW10	
12 S 20	Motcomb st SW1	
6 Z 14	Mount mills EC1	
1 C 2	Mount Pleasant rd NW10	
6 R 17	Mount pleasant WC1	
6 R 18	Mount pleasant WC1	
12 W 10	Mount row W1	
12 W 10	Mount st W1	
16 V 2	Mount ter E1	
6 R 1	Mountford ter N1	
8 Y 7	Mowlem st E2	
22 S 20	Mowll st SW9	
12 T 2	Moxon st W1	
17 M 15	Moylan rd W6	
2 O 14	Mozart st W10	
10 S 3	Mulberry st E1	
19 G 12	Mulberry wlk SW3	
17 O 14	Mulgrave rd W14	
3 J 18	Mulready st NW8	
18 P 11	Mund st W14	
17 K 6	Munden st W14	
1 M 20	Munro ms W10	
4 Z 15	Munster sq NW1	
23 D 5	Munton rd SE17	
6 P 7	Muriel st N1	
14 S 19	Murphy st SE1	
7 E 10	Murray gro N1	
17 L 14	Musard rd W6	
15 L 9	Muscovy st EC3	
13 J 2	Museum st WC1	
18 V 20	Musgrave cres SW6	
2 V 3	Mutrix rd NW6	
6 T 12	Myddelton pas EC1	
6 T 11	Myddelton sq EC1	
6 U 14	Myddelton st EC1	
6 T 11	Mylne st EC1	
16 U 4	Myrdle st E1	
J 10	Myrtle st N1	

N

7 B 17	Nags Head ct EC1	
18 N 1	Napier clo W14	
7 C 9	Napier gro N1	
18 O 2	Napier pl W14	
18 N 2	Napier rd W14	
6 V 3	Napier ter N1	
9 B 5	Nascot st W12	
13 B 2	Nassau st W1	
14 P 13	National Film theatre SE1	

13 H 11 National Gallery WC2
13 H 11 National Portrait Gallery WC2
14 R 13 National Theatre SE1
19 F 3 Natural History museum SW7
7 M 15 Navarre st E2
24 W 18 Naylor rd SE15
13 J 6 Neal st WC2
13 J 6 Neals yd WC2
23 K 14 Neate st SE5
24 O 14 Neate st SE5
21 A 4 Neathouse pl SW1
15 D 19 Nebraska st SE1
24 O 1 Neckinger SE16
10 T 6 Needham rd W11
17 F 14 Nella rd W6
24 Z 6 Nelldale rd SE16
6 X 10 Nelson pl N1
14 X 16 Nelson sq SE1
16 W 4 Nelson st E1
6 X 10 Nelson ter N1
24 S 2 Ness st SE16
19 C 15 Netherton gro SW10
9 F 20 Netherwood pl W14
9 F 20 Netherwood rd W14
5 A 14 Netley st SW1
18 T 7 Nevern pl SW5
18 T 7 Nevern rd SW5
18 T 7 Nevern st SW5
5 G 9 Neville clo NW1
2 R 10 Neville clo NW6
2 S 9 Neville st SW7
19 F 9 Neville st SW7
19 F 9 Neville ter SW7
12 Y 7 New Bond st W1
12 Z 10 New Bond st W1
14 W 7 New Br st EC4
13 A 9 New Burlington ms W1
13 A 8 New Burlington pl W1
13 A 9 New Burlington st W1
12 X 1 New Cavendish st W1
15 A 6 New Change EC4
23 F 16 New Church rd SE5
23 D 18 New Church rd SE5
13 H 5 New Compton st WC2
21 D 20 New Covent Garden market SW8
13 G 10 New Coventry st W1
14 R 8 New ct WC2
14 U 3 New Fetter la EC4
15 H 11 New Fresh wharf EC3
16 N 4 New Goulston st E1
7 L 15 New Inn sq EC2
7 K 15 New Inn st EC2
7 K 16 New Inn yd EC2
23 D 4 New Kent rd SE1
15 L 8 New London st EC3
7 J 17 New North pl EC2
7 F 9 New North rd N1
5 M 20 New North st WC1
13 H 4 New Oxford st WC1
13 K 19 New Palace yd SW1
24 W 1 New Place sq SE16
12 R 6 New Quebec st W1
16 V 4 New rd E1
13 J 9 New row WC2
21 F 1 New Scotland yd SW1
21 M 11 New Spring Gardens wlk SE11
14 R 5 New sq WC2
15 K 3 New st EC2
14 U 4 New St sq EC4
15 E 1 New Union st EC2
5 M 8 New Wharf rd N1

16 W 2 Newark st E1
13 B 7 Newburgh st W1
22 P 9 Newburn st SE11
14 Z 1 Newbury st EC1
14 W 4 Newcastle clo EC4
11 H 1 Newcastle pl W2
6 U 16 Newcastle row EC1
10 U 13 Newcombe st W8
15 E 16 Newcomen st SE11
3 K 10 Newcourt st NW8
23 J 16 Newent clo SE15
14 X 4 Newgate st EC1
22 Y 6 Newington Butts SE11
22 Z 2 Newington causeway SE1
13 D 3 Newman pas W1
14 P 3 Newmans row WC2
13 C 2 Newmans st W1
22 R 1 Newnham ter SE1
14 R 20 Newnham ter SE1
15 L 20 Newnhams row SE1
13 G 8 Newport ct WC2
13 G 8 Newport pl WC2
22 O 6 Newport st SE11
7 H 7 Newton gro N1
10 W 5 Newton rd W2
13 M 4 Newton st WC2
8 S 7 Nicholl st E2
14 X 14 Nicholson st SE1
7 D 12 Nile st N1
24 O 12 Nile ter SE15
21 H 15 Nine Elms la SW8
17 F 18 Niton st SW6
6 X 8 Noel rd N1
13 C 6 Noel st W1
9 J 2 Norburn st W10
11 L 5 Norfolk cres W2
11 H 5 Norfolk pl W2
3 J 5 Norfolk rd NW8
22 O 4 Norfolk row SE11
11 G 6 Norfolk Sq Ms W2
11 G 5 Norfolk sq W2
17 K 12 Norfolk ter W6
9 L 14 Norland rd W11
9 H 15 Norland pl W11
9 L 14 Norland sq W11
7 B 15 Norman st EC1
17 M 13 Normand ms W14
18 N 15 Normand pk W14
18 N 13 Normand rd W14
13 E 11 Norris st SW1
12 T 8 North Audley st W1
5 M 9 North av N1
3 J 14 North Bank NW8
5 E 20 North cres WC1
5 C 20 North ct W1
18 N 7 North End cres W14
17 L 5 North End rd SW6
18 R 13 North End rd W14
5 B 14 North Gower st NW1
6 P 18 North ms WC1
9 B 3 North Pole rd W10
12 T 7 North row W1
16 P 6 North Tenter st E1
19 J 4 North ter SW3
11 F 3 North Wharf rd W2
6 T 16 Northampton rd EC1
6 T 16 Northampton row EC1
6 X 13 Northampton sq EC1
6 X 17 Northburgh st EC1
7 J 1 Northchurch ter N1
5 M 10 Northdown st N1
8 Y 6 Northiam st E9
6 P 19 Northington st WC1
7 H 7 Northport st N1
15 M 7 Northumberland all EC3
13 K 13 Northumberland av WC2
10 U 5 Northumberland pl W2

13 J 12 Northumberland st WC2
3 F 17 Northwick clo NW8
3 E 17 Northwick ter NW8
7 L 19 Norton folgate E1
14 T 3 Norwich st EC4
23 E 18 Notley st SE5
10 T 12 Notting Hill ga W11
13 K 6 Nottingham ct WC2
4 T 19 Nottingham pl W1
4 T 20 Nottingham st W1
3 C 11 Nugent ter NW8
9 B 2 Nursery la W10
1 K 12 Nutbourne st W10
23 V 18 Nutcroft rd SE16
12 N 4 Nutford pl W1
24 P 18 Nutt st SE15
7 L 7 Nuttall st N1

O

15 C 15 O'meara st SE1
3 J 14 Oak Tree rd NW8
22 U 6 Oakden st SE11
19 A 13 Oakfields st SW10
2 U 17 Oakington rd W9
6 X 10 Oakley cres N1
19 L 13 Oakley gdns SW3
24 N 11 Oakley pl SE1
5 C 8 Oakley sq NW1
19 K 14 Oakley st SW3
17 J 14 Oakley wk W6
18 O 1 Oakwood ct W14
10 O 20 Oakwood la W14
9 E 1 Oakworth rd W10
10 U 17 Observatory gdns W8
23 A 9 Occupation rd SE17
22 S 18 Offley rd SW9
13 A 1 Ogle st W1
2 E 6 Okehampton rd SW10
9 G 11 Olaf st W11
14 X 5 Old Bailey EC4
5 T 18 Old Barrack yd SW1
8 T 12 Old Bethnal Green rd E2
14 R 4 Old bldgs WC2
13 A 12 Old Bond st W1
15 H 3 Old Broad st EC2
19 B 9 Old Brompton rd SW5
13 A 10 Old Burlington st W1
16 O 4 Old Castle st E1
12 X 5 Old Cavendish st W1
19 J 15 Old Church st SW3
13 E 8 Old Compton st W1
10 X 17 Old Ct pl W8
8 Z 11 Old Ford rd E2
13 M 1 Old Gloucester st WC1
5 L 20 Old Gloucester st WC1
24 R 1 Old Jamaica rd SE16
15 D 6 Old Jewry EC2
23 K 7 Old Kent rd SE1
24 X 16 Old Kent rd SE15
18 W 8 Old Manor st SW5
11 L 2 Old Marylebone rd NW1
14 T 17 Old Mitre ct EC4
16 R 2 Old Montague st E1
8 U 20 Old Montague st E1
7 M 15 Old Nichol st E2
8 N 15 Old Nichol st E2
14 N 1 Old North st WC1
22 O 5 Old Paradise st SE11

12 W 16	Old Park la W1
21 F 1	Old Pye st SW1
12 R 7	Old Quebec st W1
13 G 19	Old Queen st SW1
14 W 5	Old Seacoal la EC4
21 L 18	Old South Lambeth rd SW8
14 R 4	Old sq WC2
7 J 14	Old st EC1
4 T 19	Oldbury pl W1
1 K 11	Oliphant st W10
7 F 17	Olivers yd EC2
24 R 13	Olmar st SE1
23 A 14	Olney rd SE17
22 Z 14	Olney st SE17
17 M 3	Olympia rd W14
17 L 4	Olympia W14
10 Z 9	Olympia yd W2
5 M 10	Omega pl N1
18 T 13	Ongar rd SW6
19 E 8	Onslow gdns SW7
19 F 7	Onslow Ms east SW7
19 E 8	Onslow Ms west SW7
19 G 6	Onslow sq SW7
6 U 19	Onslow st EC1
22 Y 2	Ontario st SE1
22 V 9	Opal st SE11
4 O 2	Oppidans rd NW3
4 O 1	Oppidans rd NW3
13 F 11	Orange st WC2
13 G 6	Orange yd W1
23 E 8	Orb st SE17
17 M 19	Orbain rd SW6
12 T 8	Orchard st W1
3 F 18	Orchardson st NW8
6 N 19	Orde Hall st WC1
3 G 6	Ordnance hill NW8
3 H 8	Ordnance ms NW8
22 W 4	Orient st SE11
10 Y 10	Orme Ct ms W2
10 Y 9	Orme ct W2
10 X 10	Orme la W2
10 X 10	Orme sq W2
5 M 18	Ormond ms WC1
13 C 12	Ormond yd SW1
20 O 11	Ormonde ga SW3
4 O 6	Ormonde ter NW8
8 N 8	Ormsby st E2
10 Z 4	Orsett ms W2
10 Z 4	Orsett ms W2
11 A 4	Orsett ms W2
22 P 9	Orsett st SE11
10 Z 4	Orsett ter W2
11 A 4	Orsett ter W2
7 L 5	Orsman rd N1
16 T 14	Orton st E1
21 E 7	Osbert st SW1
8 S 5	Osborn clo E8
16 P 3	Osborn st E1
4 Z 16	Osnaburgh st NW1
4 Z 17	Osnaburgh ter NW1
12 T 1	Ossington bldgs W1
10 W 11	Ossington st W2
24 R 12	Ossory rd SE1
5 F 11	Ossulston st NW1
18 Z 3	Osten ms SW7
22 X 4	Oswin st SE11
22 W 9	Othello clo SE11
22 W 14	Otto st SE17
3 M 11	Outer circle NW1 & NW8
4 W 10	Outer circle NW1 & NW8
5 L 4	Outram st N1
15 K 4	Outwhich st EC3
22 R 14	Oval Cricket grd SE11
4 X 5	Oval rd NW1
8 W 8	Oval the E2
22 P 12	Oval way SE11
17 B 5	Overstone rd W6
19 L 2	Ovington gdns SW3
19 M 2	Ovington ms SW3

19 M 2	Ovington sq SW3
19 M 4	Ovington st SW3
20 N 5	Ovington st SW3
6 V 11	Owens ct EC1
6 W 11	Owens ct EC1
6 V 11	Owens row EC1
13 F 10	Oxendon st SW1
13 A 6	Oxford Cir av W1
13 A 6	Oxford cir W1
9 J 4	Oxford gdns W10
2 W 7	Oxford rd NW6
11 L 6	Oxford sq W2
13 E 4	Oxford st W1
12 T 17	Oxford st W1

P

16 Y 7	Paoo pl E1
7 A 6	Packington sq N1
6 Y 4	Packington st N1
8 P 14	Padbury ct E2
11 G 1	Paddington grn W2
12 S 1	Paddington st W1
11 F 6	Paddington station W2
21 G 5	Page st SW1
23 L 3	Pages wlk SE1
6 W 12	Paget st EC1
6 P 15	Pakenham st WC1
10 Z 17	Palace av W8
10 W 10	Palace ct W2
11 B 19	Palace ga W8
10 W 12	Palace Gdns ms W8
10 W 14	Palace Gdns ter W8
10 Y 17	Palace gen W8
20 U 7	Palace ms SW1
21 B 2	Palace st SW1
22 R 17	Palfrey pl SW8
8 O 14	Palissy st E2
13 G 13	Pall Mall east SW1
13 C 14	Pall Mall pl SW1
13 E 14	Pall Mall SW1
17 K 10	Palliser rd W14
3 G 16	Pallitt dri NW8
13 D 20	Palmer st SW1
21 E 1	Palmer st SW1
9 F 6	Pamber st W10
5 V 14	Pancras rd NW1
9 D 1	Pangbourne av W10
13 G 10	Panton st WC2
14 T 8	Paper bldng EC4
20 S 16	Parade the SW11
16 Y 19	Paradise st SE16
20 P 13	Paradise wlk SW3
6 Y 16	Pardon st EC1
15 G 20	Pardoner st SE1
16 U 4	Parfett st E1
17 E 13	Parfrey st W6
14 V 13	Paris gdn SE1
4 W 19	Park Cres Ms east W1
4 Y 18	Park Cres Ms east W1
4 X 18	Park cres W1
13 B 14	Park pl SW1
3 D 20	Park Pl vlls W2
4 O 17	Park rd NW1
3 L 13	Park rd NW8
4 X 17	Park Sq east NW1
4 W 17	Park Sq ms NW1
4 W 17	Park Sq west NW1
15 B 12	Park st SE1
12 S 7	Park st W1
12 T 11	Park st W1
4 Y 9	Park Village east NW1
4 X 8	Park Village west NW1
11 L 5	Park West pl W2
19 D 13	Park wlk SW10
13 M 4	Parker st WC2

16 R 19	Parkers row SE1
6 U 8	Parkfield st N1
19 K 20	Parkgate rd SW11
23 G 17	Parkhouse st SE5
18 O 19	Parkville rd SW6
4 X 5	Parkway NW1
13 J 19	Parliament sq SW1
13 J 18	Parliament st SW1
8 Y 8	Parmiter pl E2
8 Y 9	Parmiter st E2
7 D 7	Parr st N1
21 K 14	Parry st SW8
21 H 18	Pascal st SW8
20 T 8	Passmore st SW1
22 Y 4	Pastor st SE11
18 T 2	Pater st W8
14 Y 5	Paternoster sq EC4
22 W 20	Patmos rd SW9
7 A 14	Paton st EC1
8 Y 10	Patriot sq E2
7 H 18	Paul st EC2
19 H 14	Paultons sq SW3
19 H 15	Paultons st SW3
19 J 19	Paveley dr SW11
3 L 15	Paveley st NW8
12 P 20	Pavilion rd SW1
20 P 4	Pavilion rd SW1
20 P 3	Pavilion st SW1
17 K 14	Paynes wk W6
20 X 10	Peabody av SW1
20 Y 12	Peabody clo SW1
21 F 11	Peabody estate SW1
8 T 17	Peace st E1
22 Y 8	Peacock st SE17
22 Z 8	Peacock yd SE17
14 T 17	Pear pl SE1
6 U 17	Pear Tree ct EC1
7 A 15	Pear Tree st EC1
6 Z 15	Pear Tree st EC1
14 T 19	Pearman st SE1
8 N 8	Pearson st E2
7 M 8	Pearson st E2
23 K 18	Peckham gro SE15
24 R 19	Peckham Hill st SE15
24 U 14	Peckham Pk rd SE15
8 S 10	Peel Precinct ct NW6
10 U 14	Peel st W8
7 E 14	Peerless st EC1
22 S 13	Pegasus pl SE11
19 J 7	Pelham cres SW7
19 J 6	Pelham pl SW7
19 J 6	Pelham st SW7
23 B 13	Pelier st SE17
17 M 16	Pellant rd SW6
8 N 12	Pelter st E2
1 F 13	Pember rd NW10
14 U 5	Pemberton row EC4
10 S 9	Pembridge cres W11
10 U 11	Pembridge gdns W2
10 S 9	Pembridge ms W11
10 U 8	Pembridge pl W2
10 T 10	Pembridge rd W11
10 U 9	Pembridge sq W2
10 T 8	Pembridge vlls W11
12 U 18	Pembroke clo SW1
18 S 4	Pembroke Gdns clo W8
18 S 5	Pembroke gdns W8
18 T 3	Pembroke ms W8
18 T 2	Pembroke pl W8
18 R 6	Pembroke rd W14
18 T 4	Pembroke sq W8
5 M 3	Pembroke st N1
18 R 3	Pembroke studios W8
18 T 4	Pembroke vlls W8
18 T 4	Pembroke wlk W8
7 F 4	Penally pl N1
16 Y 12	Penang st E1
24 V 15	Pencraig way SE15
3 J 20	Penfold pl NW1

3 H 19 Penfold pl NW8
7 G 5 Penn st N1
18 X 4 Pennant ms W8
9 C 16 Pennard rd W12
24 V 20 Pennethorne rd SE15
16 V 11 Pennington st E1
23 A 11 Penrose gro SE17
23 A 10 Penrose st SE17
23 A 12 Penrose st SE17
23 L 8 Penry st SE1
5 E 8 Penryn st SW1
6 S 9 Penton gro N1
22 X 8 Penton pl SE17
23 A 10 Penton pl SE17
6 P 11 Penton ri WC1
6 S 9 Penton st N1
6 R 10 Pentonville rd N1
23 M 20 Pentridge st SE15
18 V 9 Penywern rd SW5
9 L 12 Penzance pl W11
9 L 13 Penzance st W11
1 H 9 Peploe rd NW6
15 A 16 Pepper st SE1
15 L 9 Pepys st EC3
6 W 15 Percival st EC1
6 P 12 Percy cir WC1
13 E 3 Percy ms W1
13 E 2 Percy st W1
6 P 13 Percy yd WC1
17 M 12 Perham rd W14
18 N 12 Perham rd W14
21 F 2 Perkins rents SW1
13 E 4 Perrys pl W1
13 E 7 Peter st W1
14 Z 7 Peters hill EC4
6 X 20 Peters la EC1
19 B 1 Petersham la SW7
19 B 2 Petersham ms SW7
19 B 2 Petersham pl SW7
17 E 16 Petley rd W6
4 Y 17 Peto pl NW1
15 M 4 Petticoat la E1
13 D 20 Petty France SW1
19 J 15 Petyt pl SW3
19 M 7 Petyward SW3
23 E 13 Phelp st SE17
19 L 14 Phene st SW3
18 T 9 Philbeach gdns SW5
16 T 7 Philchurch pl E1
1 B 4 Phillimore gdns NW10
10 S 19 Phillimore gdns W8
10 T 19 Phillimore pl W8
10 T 20 Phillimore wlk W8
7 L 6 Phillipp st N1
15 H 9 Philpot la EC3
16 X 4 Philpot st E1
7 J 17 Phipp st EC2
20 X 4 Phipps ms SW1
6 R 16 Phoenix pl WC1
5 G 10 Phoenix rd NW1
13 H 6 Phoenix st WC2
13 B 12 Piccadilly arc SW1
13 E 10 Piccadilly cir W1
13 C 11 Piccadilly pl W1
12 Y 14 Piccadilly W1
13 B 12 Piccadilly W1
6 Z 12 Pickard st EC1
10 Y 5 Pickering ms W2
6 Z 3 Pickering st N1
15 L 14 Pickle Herring st SE1
15 B 18 Pickwick st SE1
21 L 20 Pickworth clo SW8
12 U 6 Picton pl W1
23 F 19 Picton st SE5
6 W 7 Pierrepont row N1
14 W 6 Pilgrim st EC4
15 F 19 Pilgrimage st SE1
23 C 9 Pilton pl SE17
21 E 13 Pimlico gdns SW1
20 U 8 Pimlico rd SW1

16 T 8 Pinchin st E1
7 K 20 Pindar st EC2
2 Z 17 Pindock ms W9
6 T 16 Pine st EC1
7 H 14 Pitfield st N1
23 A 18 Pitman st SE5
10 V 17 Pitt st W8
15 K 14 Pitts ct SE1
12 V 14 Pitts Head ms W1
15 F 18 Plaintain pl SE1
7 G 17 Platina st EC2
5 F 9 Platt st NW1
17 E 12 Playfair st W6
14 X 8 Playhouse yd EC4
6 Z 2 Pleasant pl N1
4 Z 5 Pleasant row NW1
5 B 6 Plender pl NW1
5 B 6 Plender sy NW1
14 U 6 Pleydell ct EC4
14 U 6 Pleydell st EC4
14 T 4 Plough pl EC4
7 K 18 Plough yd EC2
6 U 15 Plumbers pl EC1
16 T 3 Plumbers row E1
14 V 3 Plumtree ct EC4
2 N 2 Plympton av NW6
3 K 18 Plympton pl NW8
2 O 1 Plympton rd NW6
3 K 18 Plympton st NW8
14 X 17 Pocock st SE1
13 C 5 Poland st W1
8 U 13 Pollard row E2
8 U 13 Pollard st E2
12 Z 7 Pollen st W1
5 D 11 Polygon rd NW1
19 J 8 Pond pl SW3
16 V 7 Ponler st E1
21 H 9 Ponsonby pl SW1
21 H 9 Ponsonby ter SW1
20 N 2 Pont St ms SW3
20 R 2 Pont st SW1
21 F 16 Ponton rd SW8
14 V 17 Pontypool pl SE1
7 E 6 Poole st N1
19 B 20 Pooles la SW10
15 M 19 Pope st SE1
7 A 3 Popham rd N1
6 Y 4 Popham st N1
7 A 4 Popham st N1
9 D 20 Poplar gro W6
10 Y 9 Poplar pl W2
14 V 5 Poppins ct EC4
10 Z 4 Porchester ms W2
11 L 6 Porchester pl W2
10 Y 5 Porchester rd W2
10 Y 4 Porchester sq W2
11 K 4 Porchester st W2
10 Z 3 Porchester Ter north W2
11 B 10 Porchester ter W2
15 F 18 Porlock st SE1
17 J 2 Porten rd W14
4 R 20 Porter st W1
11 E 1 Porteus rd W2
2 P 15 Portgate clo W9
13 C 7 Portland ms W1
4 Y 19 Portland pl W1
12 Y 1 Portland pl W1
9 M 12 Portland rd W11
23 E 11 Portland st SE17
12 S 4 Portman clo W1
12 S 6 Portman Ms south W1
12 S 6 Portman sq W1
12 R 6 Portman st W1
2 O 11 Portnall rd W9
10 T 10 Portobello ms W11
9 M 2 Portobello rd W10
1 K 19 Portobello rd W11
10 T 10 Portobello rd W11
6 S 20 Portpool la EC1
11 M 6 Portsea ms W2
11 M 6 Portsea pl W2

14 O 5 Portsmouth st WC2
16 O 8 Portsoken st E1
14 P 5 Portugal st WC2
21 F 16 Post office way SW8
23 G 2 Potier st SE1
8 X 14 Pott st E2
15 L 15 Potters fields SE1
9 L 12 Pottery la W11
16 V 18 Pottery st SE16
15 D 6 Poultry EC2
10 P 5 Powis gdns W11
9 R 5 Powis ms W11
5 L 19 Powis pl WC1
10 R 6 Powis sq W11
10 R 5 Powis ter W11
8 R 5 Pownall rd E8
8 Y 11 Poyser st E2
11 G 5 Praed ms W2
11 F 6 Praed st W2
5 A 5 Pratt ms NW1
5 C 3 Pratt st NW1
22 O 4 Pratt wlk SE11
7 B 5 Prebend st N1
16 O 8 Prescott st E1
7 A 13 President st EC1
23 J 6 Preston clo SE1
14 Y 14 Prices st SE1
6 O 4 Prices yd N1
6 R 12 Prideaux pl WC1
22 T 17 Prima rd SW9
14 V 7 Primrose hill EC4
4 N 1 Primrose Hill rd NW3
4 S 3 Primrose Hill stds NW1
7 K 20 Primrose st EC2
3 K 11 Prince Albert rd NW1
4 P 6 Prince Albert rd NW1
11 E 20 Prince Consort rd SW7
20 W 20 Prince of Wales dri SW8
10 Z 19 Prince of Wales ter W8
20 Y 20 Prince of Wales dri SW11
9 L 13 Princedale rd W11
8 P 20 Princelet st E1
13 C 12 Princes arc SW1
19 H 2 Princes Ga ms SW7
11 G 19 Princes ga SW7
11 K 19 Princes ga SW7
19 H 1 Princes gdns SW7
11 H 20 Princes gdns SW7
10 W 9 Princes ms W2
13 C 13 Princes pl SW1
9 L 13 Princes pl W11
10 W 8 Princes sq W2
15 E 5 Princes st EC2
12 Z 6 Princes st W1
4 U 3 Princess rd NW1
2 U 9 Princess rd NW6
12 Y 3 Princess st SE1
14 N 1 Princeton st WC1
14 U 4 Printers st EC4
14 X 8 Printing House sq EC4
23 G 3 Prioress st SE1
2 P 4 Priory Pk rd NW6
2 X 1 Priory rd NW6
2 X 4 Priory ter NW6
19 C 11 Priory wlk SW10
8 V 8 Pritchards rd E2
24 T 2 Priter rd SE16
24 T 3 Priter way SE16
14 N 2 Procter st WC1
16 X 20 Prospect st SE16
18 N 17 Prothero rd SW6
7 A 8 Provence st N1
12 U 8 Providence ct W1

6 V 5 Providence pl N1
7 E 12 Provost st N1
5 A 1 Prowse pl NW1
16 Z 12 Prusom st E1
14 X 9 Puddle dock EC4
6 R 5 Pulteney ter N1
18 T 19 Pulton pl SW6
8 O 20 Puma ct E1
14 S 7 Pump ct EC4
8 X 12 Pundersons gdns E2
15 M 20 Purbrook st SE1
17 J 17 Purcell cres SW6
7 J 9 Purcell st N1
5 G 9 Purchese st NW1
1 C 10 Purves rd NW10

Q

8 N 18 Quaker st E1
14 S 4 Quality ct WC2
12 P 6 Quebec ms W1
12 Y 3 Queen Anne ms W1
12 X 3 Queen Anne st W1
13 F 19 Queen Annes ga SW1
17 C 10 Queen Caroline st W6
14 P 13 Queen Elizabeth hall SE1
16 O 17 Queen Elizabeth st SE1
4 S 15 Queen Marys gdns NW1
5 K 19 Queen Sq pl WC1
5 K 19 Queen sq WC1
15 C 9 Queen st EC4
12 X 13 Queen st Mayfair W1
15 C 10 Queen St pl EC4
14 Y 8 Queen Victoria st EC4
15 B 8 Queen Victoria st EC4
20 X 20 Queens cir SW11
18 N 13 Queens Club gdns W14
17 M 13 Queens Club gdns W14
17 L 12 Queens Club the W14
19 G 11 Queens Elm sq SW3
19 B 3 Queens Ga gdns SW7
19 B 1 Queens Ga ms SW7
19 D 4 Queens Ga Pl ms SW7
19 D 3 Queens Ga pl SW7
19 D 3 Queens ga SW7
11 D 20 Queens ga SW7
19 C 1 Queens Ga ter SW7
12 Z 19 Queens Gallery SW1
11 C 20 Queens Gate ms SW7
11 B 8 Queens gdns W2
3 F 7 Queens gro NW8
6 Y 5 Queens Head st N1
15 E 15 Queens Head yd SE1
10 Y 8 Queens ms W2
1 K 7 Queens pk NW6
20 V 18 Queens rd SW11
23 D 13 Queens row SE17
3 F 7 Queens ter NW8
19 E 5 Queensberry Ms west SW7
19 E 5 Queensberry pl SW7
19 F 5 Queensberry way SW7
11 A 8 Queensborough pas W2
11 A 10 Queensborough ter W2
8 P 3 Queensbridge rd E8
7 C 2 Queensbury st N1

9 H 13 Queensdale cres W11
9 J 14 Queensdale pl W11
9 H 15 Queensdale rd W11
9 K 14 Queensdale wlk W11
17 G 19 Queensmill rd SW6
20 W 17 Queenstown rd SW8
10 Y 6 Queensway W2
2 U 4 Quex ms NW6
2 V 3 Quex rd NW6
6 X 5 Quick pl N1
6 X 9 Quick st N1
3 M 1 Quickswood NW3
15 B 17 Quilp st SE1
8 R 12 Quilter st E2

R

10 V 12 Rabbit row W8
18 S 15 Racton rd SW6
22 U 11 Radcot st SE11
10 N 2 Raddington rd W10
3 K 5 Radlett pl NW8
18 V 4 Radley ms W8
11 H 6 Radnor ms W2
11 J 6 Radnor pl W2
1 L 5 Radnor rd NW6
24 S 17 Radnor rd SE15
7 C 14 Radnor st EC1
18 O 4 Radnor ter W14
19 M 11 Radnor wlk SW3
20 N 13 Radnor wlk SW3
24 T 13 Radsley st SE1
19 K 19 Radstock st SW11
15 F 14 Railway appr SE1
9 L 5 Railway ms W10
15 L 8 Railway pl EC3
5 L 9 Railway st N1
23 J 17 Rainbow st SE5
16 Y 12 Raine st E1
1 D 13 Rainham rd NW10
11 J 4 Rainsford st W2
17 E 16 Rainville rd W6
6 Z 6 Raleigh st N1
23 C 2 Ralph st SE1
13 B 5 Ramillies pl W1
13 B 6 Ramillies st W1
21 F 9 Rampayne st SW1
8 T 16 Ramsey st E2
22 N 8 Randall rd SE11
22 N 8 Randall row SE11
5 L 3 Randells rd N1
2 Z 12 Randolph av W9
3 C 17 Randolph av W9
3 B 17 Randolph cres W9
2 X 10 Randolph gdns NW6
3 C 18 Randolph ms W9
3 C 18 Randolph rd W9
5 B 1 Randolph st NW1
20 V 9 Ranelagh gro SW1
21 C 11 Ranelagh rd SW1
15 M 7 Rangoon st EC3
17 D 13 Rannoch rd W6
17 E 16 Rannoch rd W6
3 K 20 Ranston st NW1
12 N 19 Raphael st SW7
7 C 14 Ratcliff gro EC1
13 E 3 Rathbone pl W1
13 D 2 Rathbone st W1
16 X 1 Raven row E1
8 P 10 Ravenscroft st E2
22 U 11 Ravensdon st SE11
22 P 5 Ravent rd SE11
7 J 16 Ravey st EC2
20 N 6 Rawlings st SW3
6 W 12 Rawstone pl EC1
6 W 12 Rawstorne st EC1
6 U 18 Ray st EC1
24 Y 6 Raymouth rd SE16
16 X 15 Reardon path E1

16 X 13 Reardon st E1
7 A 5 Rector st N1
14 U 5 Red Lion ct EC4
23 D 14 Red Lion row SE17
14 N 2 Red Lion sq WC1
14 O 2 Red Lion st WC1
12 W 13 Red Lion yd W1
12 T 8 Red pl W1
10 Y 6 Redan pl W2
16 G 1 Redan st W14
19 H 15 Redanchor clo SW3
23 K 20 Redbridge gdns SE5
20 N 12 Redburn st SW3
23 A 19 Redcar st SE5
8 N 16 Redchurch st E2
18 W 10 Redcliffe clo SW5
19 B 14 Redcliffe gdns SW10
18 Y 10 Redcliffe gdns SW10
18 Z 12 Redcliffe ms SW10
19 A 15 Redcliffe pl SW10
19 C 13 Redcliffe rd SW10
19 Z 11 Redcliffe sq SW10
19 Z 13 Redcliffe st SW10
15 C 15 Redcross way SE1
15 D 14 Redcross wlk SE1
24 R 16 Reddins rd SE15
10 V 8 Rede pl W2
19 M 12 Redesdale st SW3
18 V 6 Redfield la SW5
6 Z 4 Redford wlk N1
4 Y 11 Redhill st NW1
24 U 10 Redlaw way SE16
16 S 14 Redmead la E1
7 L 11 Redvers st E2
19 E 6 Reece ms SW7
19 T 7 Reedworth st SE11
7 D 5 Rees st N1
12 U 10 Reeves ms W1
4 V 5 Regal la NW1
7 J 9 Regan way N1
21 F 4 Regency pl SW1
21 F 8 Regency st SW1
13 C 9 Regent pl W1
5 L 14 Regent sq WC1
1 G 14 Regent st NW10
12 Z 4 Regent st W1
13 B 10 Regent st W1
3 D 9 Regents ms NW8
4 T 8 Regents Pk Zoological gdns NW1
4 U 4 Regents Pk rd NW1
4 W 4 Regents Pk ter NW1
5 C 15 Regnart bldgs NW1
9 D 12 Relay rd W12
19 L 1 Relton ms SW7
20 S 8 Rembrandt clo SW1
6 Y 10 Remington st N1
14 N 4 Remnant st WC2
22 W 6 Renfrew rd SE11
14 V 12 Rennie st SE1
23 H 3 Rephidim st SE1
17 M 20 Repton rd SW6
11 B 20 Reston pl SW7
7 L 11 Retford st E2
24 R 6 Reverdy rd SE1
19 A 19 Rewell st SW6
12 U 11 Rex pl W1
6 Z 7 Rheidol ter N1
8 O 15 Rhode st E2
16 W 7 Richard st E1
19 M 5 Richards pl SW3
5 A 19 Richardsons ms W1
6 N 20 Richbell pl WC1
22 P 18 Richbourne ter SW8
9 B 19 Richford st W6
17 B 1 Richford st W6
6 O 3 Richmond av N1
13 E 6 Richmond bldgs W1
6 X 1 Richmond gro N1
13 E 7 Richmond ms W1

13 K 17	Richmond Ter ms SW1	
13 K 16	Richmond ter SW1	
9 G 19	Richmond wat W14	
18 U 13	Rickett st SW6	
5 E 19	Ridgemount gdns WC1	
5 F 20	Ridgmount st WC1	
13 A 2	Riding House st W1	
22 U 15	Rifle ct SE11	
9 H 12	Rifle pl W11	
15 M 19	Riley rd SE1	
19 F 16	Riley st SW10	
6 R 2	Ripplevale gro N1	
14 Z 16	Risborough st SE1	
14 Y 1	Rising Sun ct EC1	
6 R 8	Risinghill st N1	
21 M 16	Rita rd SW8	
22 N 17	Rita rd SW8	
6 T 7	Ritchie st N1	
6 Z 1	River pl N1	
6 T 12	River st EC1	
17 B 11	River ter W6	
14 N 17	Riverside wlk SE1	
17 A 14	Riverview gdns SW13	
7 K 14	Rivington st EC2	
7 L 14	Rivington st EC2	
12 T 4	Robert Adam st W1	
3 D 18	Robert clo W9	
4 Y 13	Robert st NW1	
5 A 13	Robert st NW1	
13 L 11	Robert st WC2	
8 T 13	Roberta st E2	
20 T 2	Roberts ms SW1	
6 U 16	Roberts pl EC1	
20 N 13	Robinson st SW3	
8 N 14	Rochelle st E2	
21 C 5	Rochester row SW1	
21 E 4	Rochester st SW1	
23 B 2	Rockingham st SE1	
9 F 18	Rockley rd W14	
9 C 17	Rockwood pl W12	
6 Y 9	Rocliffe st N1	
12 R 2	Rodmarton st W1	
23 C 5	Rodney pl SE17	
13 J 8	Rose st WC2	
1 H 3	Rosedene NW6	
17 F 14	Rosedew rd W6	
10 U 7	Rosehart ms W11	
24 O 18	Rosemary rd SE15	
7 F 4	Rosemary st N1	
20 N 6	Rosemoor st SW3	
9 M 9	Rosmead rd W11	
6 V 15	Rosoman pl EC1	
6 T 16	Rosoman st EC1	
3 L 17	Rossmore rd NW1	
4 N 16	Rossmore rd NW1	
14 X 20	Rotary st SE1	
7 B 1	Rotherfield st N1	
24 V 11	Rotherhithe New rd SE16	
16 X 18	Rotherhithe st SE16	
6 X 4	Rothery st N1	
23 H 2	Rothsay st SE1	
4 R 3	Rothwell st NW1	
24 S 5	Rouel rd SE16	
14 U 15	Roupell st SE1	
5 B 1	Rousden st NW1	
24 R 3	Rovel rd SE16	
17 K 19	Rowallan rd SW6	
17 F 6	Rowan rd W6	
17 F 6	Rowan ter W6	
14 O 10	Rowcross pl SE1	
24 O 9	Rowcross st SE1	
2 Y 20	Rowington clo W2	
3 A 4	Rowley way NW8	
2 Z 4	Rowley way NW8	
18 V 13	Roxby pl SW6	
13 B 11	Royal Academy W1	
11 E 20	Royal Albert hall SW7	

13 A 11	Royal arc W1	
20 O 9	Royal av SW3	
5 C 3	Royal College st NW1	
9 H 15	Royal Cres ms W11	
9 J 15	Royal cres W11	
14 O 14	Royal Festival Hall SE1	
20 P 12	Royal Hospital rd SW3	
16 P 9	Royal Mint E1	
16 P 9	Royal Mint st E1	
13 F 13	Royal Opera arc SW1	
22 W 14	Royal rd SE17	
14 P 20	Royal st SE1	
24 W 15	Ruby st SE15	
24 W 13	Ruby triangle SE15	
5 K 3	Rufford st N1	
7 J 14	Rufus st EC1	
6 N 19	Rugby st WC1	
16 Z 10	Rum clo E1	
18 Y 19	Rumbold rd SW6	
9 J 9	Runcorn pl W11	
14 W 14	Running Horse yd SE1	
13 F 9	Rupert ct W1	
2 R 10	Rupert rd NW6	
13 E 8	Rupert st W1	
7 G 8	Rushton st N1	
14 Y 18	Rushworth st SE1	
13 B 15	Russell ct SW1	
9 K 20	Russell Gdns ms W14	
17 L 1	Russell gdns W14	
17 M 2	Russell rd W14	
5 J 19	Russell sq WC1	
13 M 8	Russell st WC2	
8 Z 8	Russia la E2	
23 D 17	Rust sq SE5	
9 K 5	Ruston ms W11	
21 F 4	Rutherford st SW1	
11 K 20	Rutland Ga ms SW7	
11 K 19	Rutland ga SW7	
11 L 19	Rutland Gdns ms SW7	
11 L 19	Rutland gdns SW7	
17 A 10	Rutland gro W6	
19 K 1	Rutland Ms south SW7	
19 K 1	Rutland Ms west SW7	
19 K 1	Rutland st SW7	
13 B 13	Ryder ct SW1	
13 C 13	Ryder st SW1	
13 C 12	Ryder yd SW1	
3 A 8	Ryders ter NW8	
7 C 4	Rydon st N1	
18 O 16	Rylston rd SW6	
12 O 20	Rysbrack st SW3	

S

13 B 11	Sackville st W1	
6 U 19	Saffron hill EC1	
6 U 19	Saffron st EC1	
22 P 4	Sail st SE11	
22 V 15	St. Agnes pl SE11	
18 Z 1	St. Albans gro W8	
19 A 1	St. Albans gro W8	
11 H 1	St. Albans ms W2	
6 V 5	St. Albans pl N1	
13 F 12	St. Albans pl SW1	
17 K 12	St. Albans ter W6	
15 C 2	St. Alphage gdn EC2	
14 Y 7	St. Andrews hill EC4	
4 X 16	St. Andrews pl NW1	
17 M 12	St. Andrews rd W14	
9 J 6	St. Andrews sq W11	

14 V 3	St. Andrews st EC4	
13 E 6	St. Annes ct W1	
21 G 2	St. Anns la SW1	
9 H 13	St. Anns rd W11	
21 G 1	St. Anns st SW1	
3 G 8	St. Anns ter NW8	
9 J 14	St. Anns vlls W11	
12 V 7	St. Anselms pl W1	
16 S 13	St. Anthonys clo E1	
20 V 10	St. Barnabas st SW1	
6 Z 19	St. Barts Medical school EC1	
16 N 5	St. Botolph st EC3	
14 W 7	St. Brides pas EC4	
14 V 5	St. Brides st EC4	
5 M 11	St. Chads pl WC1	
5 L 12	St. Chads st WC1	
9 K 2	St. Charles pl W10	
9 H 2	St. Charles sq W10	
1 J 20	St. Charles sq W10	
12 V 5	St. Christophers pl W1	
16 N 7	St. Clare st EC3	
14 P 6	St. Clements la WC2	
6 U 20	St. Cross st EC1	
14 U 6	St. Dunstans ct EC4	
15 J 10	St. Dunstans hill EC3	
17 F 12	St. Dunstans rd W6	
4 N 6	St. Edmunds clo NW8	
3 M 7	St. Edmunds ter NW8	
4 N 5	St. Edmunds ter NW8	
13 E 20	St. Ermins hill SW1	
2 N 20	St. Ervans rd W10	
10 O 1	St. Ervans rd W10	
14 W 20	St. Georges cir SE1	
20 Y 7	St. Georges dri SW1	
21 B 9	St. Georges dri SW1	
4 P 4	St. Georges ms NW1	
22 X 3	St. Georges rd SE1	
21 E 11	St. Georges Sq ms SW1	
21 E 11	St. Georges sq SW1	
21 D 10	St. Georges sq SW1	
12 Z 8	St. Georges st W1	
4 P 2	St. Georges ter NW1	
23 K 15	St. Georges way SE15	
24 O 15	St. Georges way SE15	
21 F 13	St. Georges Wharf SW1	
13 H 5	St. Giles High st WC2	
13 H 6	St. Giles pas WC2	
23 H 20	St. Giles rd SE5	
6 S 13	St. Helena st WC1	
9 G 4	St. Helens gdns W10	
15 J 5	St. Helens pl EC3	
1 H 4	St. Hilldas clo NW6	
9 J 13	St. James gdns W11	
13 E 11	St. James mkt SW1	
13 F 18	St. James pk SW1	
24 U 11	St. James rd SE1	
13 B 15	St. Jamess pal SW1	
13 B 14	St. Jamess pl SW1	
24 U 11	St. Jamess rd SE1	
24 T 1	St. Jamess rd SE16	
13 D 13	St. Jamess sq SW1	
13 B 13	St. Jamess st SW1	
17 C 11	St. Jamess st W6	

4 N 6	St. Jamess Ter ms NW8	
4 N 7	St. Jamess ter NW8	
6 V 17	St. Jamess wlk EC1	
21 H 4	St. Johns gdns SW1	
9 M 11	St. Johns gdns W11	
10 N 11	St. Johns gdns W11	
6 X 19	St. Johns la EC1	
10 S 7	St. Johns ms W11	
6 X 19	St. Johns path EC1	
6 W 19	St. Johns pl EC1	
6 W 18	St. Johns sq EC1	
6 W 15	St. Johns st EC1	
1 H 15	St. Johns ter W10	
3 G 7	St. Johns Wood barrack NW8	
3 K 11	St. Johns Wood High st NW8	
3 G 3	St. Johns Wood pk NW8	
3 G 14	St. Johns Wood rd NW8	
3 J 8	St. Johns Wood ter NW8	
8 X 11	St. Judes rd E2	
2 S 3	St. Julians rd NW6	
4 W 8	St. Katherines precinct NW1	
16 O 12	St. Katherines way E1	
9 L 2	St. Lawrence ter W10	
20 O 11	St. Leonards ter SW3	
20 P 10	St. Leonards ter SW3	
19 M 14	St. Loo av SW3	
10 P 4	St. Lukes ms W11	
10 P 3	St. Lukes rd W11	
19 K 9	St. Lukes st SW3	
2 O 11	St. Lukes yd W9	
13 K 19	St. Margaret st SW1	
1 A 11	St. Margarets rd NW10	
4 U 4	St. Marks cres NW1	
9 L 6	St. Marks pl W11	
1 F 20	St. Marks rd W10	
9 G 2	St. Marks rd W11	
4 T 5	St. Marks sq NW1	
16 P 7	St. Marks st E1	
5 A 4	St. Martins clo NW1	
13 H 9	St. Martins ct WC2	
13 J 9	St. Martins la WC2	
15 A 4	St. Martins le Grand EC1	
13 H 11	St. Martins pl WC2	
13 G 11	St. Martins st WC2	
18 P 2	St. Mary Abbots ter W14	
18 P 3	St. Mary Abbots pl W8	
15 J 10	St. Mary at hill EC3	
15 K 4	St. Mary Axe EC3	
16 Z 18	St. Mary Church st SE16	
22 U 5	St. Marys gdns SE11	
2 X 2	St. Marys ms NW6	
6 X 4	St. Marys path N1	
11 F 1	St. Marys sq W2	
11 E 1	St. Marys ter W2	
22 U 5	St. Marys wlk SE11	
21 F 2	St. Matthew st SW1	
8 S 15	St. Matthews row E2	
9 K 1	St. Michaels gdns W10	
11 J 3	St. Michaels st W2	
17 M 20	St. Olafs rd SW6	
22 O 11	St. Oswalds pl SE11	
21 H 7	St. Oswulf st SW1	
5 J 11	St. Pancras station NW1	
5 E 6	St. Pancras way NW1	
7 C 4	St. Paul st N1	
14 Z 6	St. Pauls Cathedral EC4	
14 Z 6	St. Pauls Church yd EC4	
8 U 11	St. Peters clo E2	
6 X 6	St. Peters st N1	
18 N 20	St. Peters ter SW6	
10 X 9	St. Petersburgh ms W2	
10 X 10	St. Petersburgh pl W2	
7 C 5	St. Philips way N1	
9 C 2	St. Quintin av W10	
3 K 5	St. Stephens clo NW8	
10 V 4	St. Stephens cres W2	
10 U 3	St. Stephens gdns W2	
10 U 3	St. Stephens ms W2	
22 N 20	St. Stephens ter SW8	
15 F 14	St. Thomas st SE1	
18 P 17	St. Thomas way SW6	
12 U 2	St. Vincent st W1	
22 N 7	Salamanca pl SE1	
21 N 7	Salamanca st SE1 & SE11	
11 J 3	Sale pl W2	
10 Y 8	Salem rd W2	
23 E 6	Salisbury clo SE17	
14 V 6	Salisbury ct EC4	
18 O 18	Salisbury ms SW6	
4 P 20	Salisbury pl W1	
23 E 6	Salisbury row SE17	
14 V 6	Salisbury sq EC4	
3 H 18	Salisbury st NW8	
2 R 12	Saltram cres NW9	
1 M 4	Salusbury rd NW6	
2 N 0	Salusbury rd NW6	
3 H 18	Samford st NW8	
16 U 14	Sampson st E1	
8 R 5	Samuel clo E8	
22 P 8	Sancroft st SE11	
15 B 18	Sanctuary st SE1	
14 T 16	Sandell st SE1	
19 A 20	Sandford rd SW6	
23 F 9	Sandford row SE17	
24 V 13	Sandgate st SE15	
14 O 2	Sandland st WC1	
5 J 14	Sandwich st WC1	
15 L 1	Sandys row E1	
6 V 16	Sans wlk EC1	
23 F 20	Sansom st SE5	
15 M 7	Saracens Head yd EC3	
7 K 12	Sarah st N1	
14 O 5	Sardinia st WC2	
15 M 9	Savage gdns EC3	
13 A 10	Saville row W1	
21 A 19	Savona st SW8	
13 M 9	Savoy bldgs WC2	
14 N 10	Savoy hill WC2	
13 M 11	Savoy pl WC2	
14 N 11	Savoy pl WC2	
14 N 10	Savoy row WC2	
14 N 10	Savoy st WC2	
14 N 10	Savoy steps WC2	
13 M 10	Savoy way WC2	
14 Z 16	Sawyer st SE1	
15 A 17	Sawyer st SE1	
23 A 4	Sayer st SE17	
13 D 1	Scala st W1	
9 G 5	Scamps ms W10	
16 W 14	Scandrett st E1	
16 P 7	Scarborough st E1	
18 X 1	Scarsdale pl W8	
18 U 3	Scarsdale vlls W8	
8 P 9	Scawfell st E2	
19 G 2	Science museum SW7	
8 O 17	Sclater st E1	
14 X 15	Scoresby st SE1	
13 K 14	Scotland pl SW1	
6 V 16	Scotswood st EC1	
3 E 14	Scott Ellis gdns NW8	
16 T 20	Scott Lidgett cres SE16	
9 A 18	Scotts rd W12	
8 P 3	Scriven st E8	
7 J 17	Scrutton st EC2	
14 X 5	Seacoal la EC4	
5 M 14	Seaford st WC1	
18 U 13	Seagrave rd SW6	
12 N 9	Searles clo SW11	
23 F 4	Searles rd SE1	
23 E 18	Sears st SE5	
6 X 14	Sebastian st EC1	
6 X 1	Sebbon st N1	
8 U 9	Sebright pas E2	
14 S 15	Secker st SE1	
2 N 15	Second av W10	
23 H 9	Sedan way SE17	
20 S 6	Sedding st SW1	
6 O 14	Seddon st WC1	
23 J 20	Sedgemoor pl SE5	
18 S 14	Sedlescombe rd SW6	
12 X 7	Sedley pl W1	
15 L 9	Seething la EC3	
6 W 16	Sekforde st EC1	
8 U 18	Selby st E1	
22 O 7	Sellon ms SE11	
5 C 5	Selous st NW1	
19 E 9	Selwood pl SW7	
19 F 10	Selwood ter SW7	
20 W 7	Semley pl SW1	
2 Y 20	Senior st W2	
14 P 5	Serle st WC2	
14 Z 7	Sermon la EC4	
24 N 5	Setchell rd SE1	
16 U 4	Settles st E1	
12 P 18	Seville st SW1	
2 W 18	Sevington st W9	
6 Z 15	Seward st EC1	
7 A 14	Seward st EC1	
12 N 3	Seymour hall W1	
12 T 5	Seymour ms W1	
12 N 4	Seymour pl W1	
12 R 6	Seymour st W1	
19 C 13	Seymour wlk SW10	
8 P 15	Shacklewell st E2	
16 P 18	Shad Thames SE1	
16 Z 7	Shadwell pl E1	
13 E 10	Shaftesbury av W1	
18 U 4	Shaftesbury ms W8	
7 D 9	Shaftesbury st N1	
20 O 3	Shafto ms SW1	
19 D 15	Shalcomb st SW10	
9 F 8	Shalfleet dri W10	
15 K 16	Shand st SE1	
3 L 8	Shannon pl SW8	
8 N 8	Shap st E2	
24 U 14	Shards sq SE15	
4 R 2	Sharpleshall st NW1	
22 W 11	Sharsted st SE17	
13 F 10	Shavers pl SW1	
19 M 11	Shawfield st SW3	
8 P 18	Sheba st E1	
6 R 4	Sheen gro N1	
8 W 5	Sheep la E8	
10 U 15	Sheffield ter W8	
10 S 17	Sheldrake pl W8	
13 J 7	Shelton st WC2	
7 K 10	Shenfield st N1	
12 X 13	Shepherd mkt W1	
12 X 14	Shepherd st W1	
7 D 12	Shepherdess pl N1	

7 B 8	Shepherdess wlk N1	
12 E 17	Shepherds Bush common W12	
9 G 18	Shepherds Bush Shopping centre W12	
12 F 17	Shepherds Bush grn W12	
9 C 16	Shepherds Bush mkt W12	
9 G 16	Shepherds Bush pl W12	
9 E 19	Shepherds Bush rd W6	
16 D 5	Shepherds Bush rd W6	
12 T 8	Shepherds pl W1	
7 C 3	Shepperton rd N1	
13 D 6	Sheraton st W1	
17 E 3	Sherborne st N1	
17 L 19	Sherbrooke rd SW6	
16 Z 6	Sheridan st E1	
20 X 9	Sherland st SW1	
13 D 9	Sherwood st W1	
11 M 1	Shillibeer pl W1	
6 X 2	Shillingford st N1	
9 B 5	Shinfield st W12	
15 H 17	Ship & Mermaid row SE1	
8 R 11	Shipton st E2	
15 H 14	Shipwright yd SE1	
2 R 15	Shirland ms W9	
2 P 14	Shirland rd W9	
6 P 4	Shirley st N1	
14 V 6	Shoe la EC4	
7 M 15	Shoreditch High st EC2	
23 M 10	Shorncliffe rd SE1	
18 R 18	Shorrolds rd SW6	
14 V 16	Short st SE1	
16 O 9	Shorter st E1	
17 G 8	Shortlands W6	
13 J 6	Shorts gdns WC2	
12 N 3	Shouldham st W1	
10 T 3	Shrewsbury ms W2	
10 T 5	Shrewsbury rd W2	
5 D 19	Shropshire pl W1	
3 L 19	Shroton st NW1	
8 R 2	Shrubland rd E8	
8 S 18	Shuttle st E1	
13 L 2	Sicilian av WC1	
4 P 18	Siddons la NW1	
22 R 2	Sidford pl SE1	
1 B 1	Sidmouth rd NW10	
5 M 15	Sidmouth st WC1	
2 W 1	Sidney Boyd ct NW6	
6 W 11	Sidney gro EC1	
16 Z 3	Sidney sq E1	
8 Z 20	Sidney st E1	
16 Z 1	Sidney st E1	
8 X 2	Sidworth st E8	
9 H 7	Silchester rd W10	
14 Y 19	Silex st SE1	
15 D 1	Silk st EC2	
13 C 8	Silver pl W1	
9 E 12	Silver rd W12	
17 F 16	Silverton rd SW6	
15 D 18	Silvester st SE1	
10 S 9	Simon clo W11	
9 H 19	Sinclair gdns W14	
9 H 19	Sinclair rd W14	
17 K 1	Sinclair rd W14	
7 G 15	Singer st EC2	
9 J 11	Sirdar rd W11	
1 J 15	Sixth av W10	
17 D 15	Skelwith rd W6	
15 A 12	Skin Mkt pl SE1	
20 T 7	Skinner pl SW1	
6 V 15	Skinner st EC1	
22 Y 2	Skipton st SE11	
23 C 19	Slade wlk SE5	
19 C 16	Slaidburn st SW10	
21 B 18	Sleaford st SW8	

13 J 8	Slingsby pl WC2	
24 X 1	Slippers pl SE16	
19 K 6	Sloane av SW3	
20 R 9	Sloane Ct east SW3	
20 R 9	Sloane Ct west SW3	
20 S 7	Sloane gdns SW1	
20 R 7	Sloane sq SW1	
12 P 19	Sloane st SW1	
20 R 4	Sloane st SW1	
20 R 5	Sloane ter SW1	
16 W 6	Sly st E1	
11 E 7	Smallbrook ms W2	
13 L 4	Smarts pl WC2	
21 J 3	Smith sq SW1	
20 N 10	Smith st SW3	
20 N 11	Smith ter SW3	
14 X 3	Smithfield st EC1	
23 L 9	Smyrks rd SE17	
2 U 2	Smyrna rd NW6	
9 C 3	Snarsgate st W10	
14 W 3	Snow hill EC1	
7 J 19	Snowden st EC2	
15 G 17	Snowsfields SE1	
14 O 4	Soane Museum WC2	
13 F 6	Soho sq W1	
13 E 5	Soho st W1	
11 J 6	Solars cres W2	
6 S 12	Soley ms WC1	
8 X 17	Somerford st E1	
5 F 9	Somers clo NW1	
14 O 9	Somerset House WC2	
10 N 19	Somerset sq W14	
23 F 13	Sondes st SE17	
8 T 4	Sotheran clo E8	
18 Z 20	Sotheron rd SW6	
17 H 4	Souldern rd W14	
9 A 10	South Africa rd W12	
12 V 12	South Audley st W1	
19 A 10	South Bolton gdns SW5	
13 F 1	South cres WC1	
20 V 6	South Eaton pl SW1	
18 S 3	South Edwardes sq W8	
18 Y 1	South End row W8	
18 X 1	South end W8	
22 S 19	South Island pl SW9	
22 O 19	South Lambeth est SW8	
21 L 13	South Lambeth pl SE1	
21 L 17	South Lambeth rd SW8	
12 W 7	South Molton la W1	
12 W 7	South Molton pas W1	
12 W 7	South Molton st W1	
19 G 10	South pde W8	
15 G 1	South pl EC2	
15 F 2	South Pl ms EC2	
14 R 1	South sq WC1	
12 T 12	South st W1	
16 P 7	South Tenter st E1	
19 J 5	South ter SW7	
11 G 4	South Wharf rd W2	
15 E 19	Southall pl SE1	
1 M 19	Southam st W10	
14 R 3	Southampton bldgs WC2	
13 L 2	Southampton pl WC1	
5 K 19	Southampton row WC1	
13 L 9	Southampton st WC2	
23 G 18	Southampton way SE5	
23 K 19	Southampton way SE5	
9 A 19	Southbrook st W12	
17 L 6	Southcombe st W14	
1 K 18	Southern row W10	
6 N 9	Southern st N1	

17 B 5	Southerton rd W6	
7 G 1	Southgate gro N1	
15 B 16	Southwark Br rd SE1	
15 C 11	Southwark br SE1	
15 A 16	Southwark gro SE1	
24 X 2	Southwark Pk rd SE16	
16 X 20	Southwark Pk rd SE16	
24 T 5	Southwark Pk rd SE16	
15 C 14	Southwark st SE1	
19 B 4	Southwell gdns SW7	
11 J 5	Southwick ms W2	
11 J 7	Southwick pl W2	
11 J 5	Southwick st W2	
24 S 2	Spa rd SE16	
24 O 2	Spa rd SE16	
6 T 15	Spafield st EC1	
12 U 3	Spanish pl W1	
18 V 7	Spear ms SW5	
5 K 14	Speedy pl WC1	
8 R 20	Spelman st E1	
16 R 1	Spelman st E1	
17 K 14	Spencer ms W6	
6 X 13	Spencer st EC1	
21 C 1	Spenser st SW1	
7 L 20	Spital sq E1	
8 R 19	Spital st E1	
7 M 20	Spitalfields mkt E1	
20 N 8	Sprimont pl SW3	
13 H 13	Spring gdns SW1	
21 M 11	Spring Gdns wlk SE11	
12 R 1	Spring ms W1	
11 F 7	Spring st W2	
17 G 2	Spring Vale ter W14	
24 X 19	Springall st SE15	
2 W 6	Springfield la NW6	
3 A 6	Springfield rd NW8	
2 W 5	Springfield wlk NW6	
13 B 19	Spur rd SW1	
23 E 1	Spurgeon st SE1	
8 T 13	Squirries st E2	
5 E 15	Sta fore ct NW1	
13 B 16	Stable Yd rd SW1	
13 B 16	Stable yd SW1	
22 S 10	Stables way SE11	
13 H 6	Stacey st WC2	
12 P 20	Stackhouse st SW3	
19 D 19	Stadium st SW10	
2 T 13	Stafford clo NW6	
13 A 20	Stafford pl SW1	
2 T 11	Stafford rd NW6	
13 A 12	Stafford st W1	
10 T 19	Stafford ter W8	
21 A 1	Stag pl SW1	
15 G 15	Stainer st SE1	
3 L 20	Stalbridge st NW1	
24 Y 3	Stalham st SE16	
18 Y 18	Stamford Bridge stadium SW6	
14 T 13	Stamford st SE1	
8 O 11	Stamp pl E2	
23 J 7	Stanford pl SE17	
18 Y 2	Stanford rd W8	
21 E 6	Stanford st SW1	
12 U 13	Stanhope ga W1	
19 D 6	Stanhope gdns SW7	
19 D 5	Stanhope Ms east SW7	
19 C 6	Stanhope Ms south SW7	
19 C 5	Stanhope Ms west SW7	
12 N 7	Stanhope pl W2	
12 W 15	Stanhope row W1	
5 A 12	Stanhope st NW1	
11 G 8	Stanhope ter W2	

18 R 11	Stanier clo W14
9 A 14	Stanlake rd W12
9 A 15	Stanlake vlls W12
22 N 16	Stanley clo SW8
10 O 9	Stanley cres W11
10 P 9	Stanley gdns W11
5 J 9	Stanley pas NW1
6 N 3	Stanmore st N1
22 U 12	Stannary pl SE11
22 U 13	Stannary st SE11
23 K 20	Stanswood gdns SE5
7 K 9	Stanway st N1
18 O 7	Stanwick rd W14
14 S 3	Staple Inn bldgs WC1
14 S 3	Staple Inn WC1
15 G 19	Staple st SE1
15 K 8	Star all EC3
18 O 12	Star rd W14
11 J 4	Star st W2
14 S 5	Star yd WC2
5 C 14	Starcross st NW1
24 X 11	Starkleigh way SE16
24 X 10	Starkleigh way SE16
1 E 9	Station ter NW10
14 Y 6	Stationers Hall ct EC4
23 D 7	Stead st SE17
8 N 4	Stean st E8
13 J 3	Stedham pl WC1
22 Z 7	Steedman st SE17
8 U 4	Stephan clo E8
13 E 3	Stephen ms W1
13 E 3	Stephen st W1
5 C 15	Stephensons way NW1
16 W 2	Stepney way E1
11 L 20	Sterling st SW7
17 E 2	Sterndale rd W14
9 F 16	Sterne st W12
15 E 19	Sterry st SE1
17 E 20	Stevenage rd SW6
7 M 20	Steward st E1
15 L 1	Steward st E1
19 J 9	Stewarts gro SW3
20 Z 20	Stewarts la SW8
21 A 20	Stewarts rd SW8
21 C 4	Stillington st SW1
14 R 3	Stone bldgs WC2
15 K 3	Stone House ct E3
14 V 4	Stonecutter st EC4
6 T 4	Stonefield st N1
9 H 10	Stoneleigh pl W11
9 H 10	Stoneleigh st W11
15 A 19	Stones End st SE1
15 M 4	Stoney la E1
15 D 13	Stoney st SE1
15 P 7	Stonor rd W14
22 Z 11	Stopford rd SE17
13 H 19	Store st WC1
13 H 19	Storeys ga SW1
24 U 3	Storks rd SE16
6 N 3	Story st N1
12 N 5	Stourcliffe st W1
13 L 10	Strand WC2
14 P 8	Strand WC2
18 O 2	Strangways ter W14
5 M 3	Stranraer way N1
12 V 6	Stratford pl W1
17 V 4	Stratford rd W8
18 V 3	Stratford studios W8
11 J 8	Strathearn pl W2
10 V 13	Strathmore gdns W8
24 T 7	Strathnairn st SE1
12 Z 13	Stratton st W1
13 H 3	Streatham st WC1
2 P 1	Streatley rd NW6
17 K 17	Strode rd SW6
8 N 12	Stronts pl E2
21 E 3	Strutton ground SW1
15 M 2	Strype st E1
2 U 14	Stuart rd NW6
4 Y 1	Stucley st NW1
6 W 4	Studd st N1
24 X 18	Studholme sr SE15
12 R 18	Studio pl SW1
13 L 4	Stukeley st WC2
14 Z 17	Sturge st SE1
22 Z 11	Sturgeon rd SE17
7 B 19	Sturt st N1
16 U 7	Stutfield st E1
6 X 9	Sudeley st N1
15 A 18	Sudrey st SE1
13 F 12	Suffolk pl SW1
13 F 12	Suffolk st SW1
23 E 16	Sugden st SE5
9 D 19	Sulgrave rd W6
17 C 1	Sulgrave rd W6
22 V 5	Sullivan rd SE11
23 A 18	Sultan st SF5
1 M 8	Summerfield av NW6
2 N 8	Summerfield av NW6
6 T 18	Summers st EC1
19 G 6	Sumner Pl ms SW7
19 G 7	Sumner pl SW7
24 O 15	Sumner rd SE15
14 Z 13	Sumner st SE1
15 A 13	Sumner st SE1
18 O 12	Sun rd W14
7 H 20	Sun st EC2
7 J 20	Sun St pas EC2
15 J 1	Sun St pas EC2
10 W 5	Sunderland ter W2
2 V 18	Surrendale pl W9
14 X 17	Surrey row SE1
23 K 8	Surrey sq SE1
4 P 8	Surrey st WC2
11 H 6	Sussex gdns W2
11 H 8	Sussex Ms east W2
11 G 9	Sussex Ms west W2
4 O 16	Sussex pl NW1
11 H 7	Sussex pl W2
17 C 9	Sussex pl W6
11 G 8	Sussex sq W2
20 Z 10	Sussex st SW1
2 V 19	Sutherland av W9
0 D 19	Sutherland av W9
10 T 5	Sutherland pl W2
20 Y 9	Sutherland row SW1
23 A 12	Sutherland sq SE17
20 Z 11	Sutherland st SW1
23 B 12	Sutherland wlk SE17
13 F 5	Sutton row W1
1 B 19	Sutton way W10
12 Z 6	Swallow pas W1
13 C 11	Swallow st W1
23 J 3	Swan mead SE1
15 C 19	Swan st SE1
15 F 11	Swan wharf EC4
20 O 14	Swan wlk SW3
8 O 15	Swanfield st E2
9 H 14	Swanscombe rd W11
16 V 9	Swedenborg gdns E1
16 O 19	Sweeney cres SE1
10 N 1	Swinbrook rd W10
9 A 14	Swindon st W12
6 N 13	Swinton pl WC1
6 O 12	Swinton st WC1
9 A 20	Sycamore gdns W6
7 A 17	Sycamore st EC1
19 H 8	Sydney clo SW3
19 H 7	Sydney ms SW3
19 H 7	Sydney pl SW7
19 J 8	Sydney st SW3
24 Y 16	Sylvan gro SE15
20 P 6	Symons st SW3

T

15 D 18	Tabard st SE1
23 F 1	Tabard st SE1
7 G 18	Tabernacle st EC2
21 B 6	Tachbrook ms SW1
21 E 9	Tachbrook st SW1
19 C 18	Tadema rd SW10
9 E 15	Tadmor st W12
10 P 6	Talbot rd W11
10 U 4	Talbot rd W2
11 G 6	Talbot sq W2
15 F 15	Talbot yd SE1
17 J 9	Talgarth rd W14
14 U 8	Tallis st EC4
2 S 16	Tamplin ms W9
18 T 14	Tamworth st SW6
5 L 13	Tankerton st WC1
16 O 18	Tanner st SE1
15 K 18	Tanner st SE1
14 T 18	Tanswell st SE1
7 B 10	Taplow st N1
8 X 17	Tapp st E1
16 Y 6	Tarling st E1
22 Y 10	Tarver rd SE17
17 K 14	Tasso rd W6
21 J 7	Tate gallery SW1
23 G 7	Tatum st SE17
4 O 18	Taunton ms NW1
4 N 17	Taunton pl NW1
9 K 15	Taverners clo W11
10 O 2	Tavistock cres W10
10 N 5	Tavistock ms W11
5 H 16	Tavistock pl WC1
10 O 3	Tavistock rd W11
5 G 16	Tavistock sq WC1
14 N 7	Tavistock st WC2
13 M 9	Tavistock st WC2
5 F 16	Taviton st WC1
5 M 2	Tayport clo N1
8 U 8	Teale st E2
20 N 11	Tedworth gdns SW3
20 N 11	Tedworth sq SW3
8 V 10	Teesdale yd E2
18 R 14	Telephone pl W14
1 K 20	Telford rd W10
14 U 8	Temple av EC4
14 U 7	Temple la EC4
14 P 9	Temple pl WC2
9 V 0	Temple st E2
8 Z 3	Templecombe rd E9
18 U 6	Templeton pl SW5
16 W 13	Tench st E1
24 V 8	Tenda rd SE16
13 B 8	Tenison ct W1
14 R 14	Tenison way SE1
11 A 8	Tenniel clo W2
15 E 17	Tennis st SE1
2 P 5	Tennyson rd SW6
8 V 17	Tent st E1
16 N 2	Tenter ground E1
12 Y 6	Tenterden st W1
20 Z 4	Terminus pl SW1
2 S 3	Terrace the NW6
20 P 16	Terrace wlk SW11
6 W 2	Terretts pl N1
6 V 6	Tetbury pl N1
24 U 10	Tetterby way SE16
10 Y 20	Thackeray st W8
5 J 14	Thanet st WC1
14 U 3	Thavies in EC4
18 R 13	Thaxton rd SW6
12 U 4	Thayer st W1
6 V 4	Theberton st N1
14 T 14	Theed st SE1
23 E 3	Theobald st SE1
6 O 20	Theobalds rd WC1
21 A 19	Thessally rd SW8
1 M 15	Third av W10
21 C 3	Thirleby rd SW1
19 C 9	Thistle gro SW5
22 X 1	Thomas Doyle st SE1
16 S 12	Thomas More st SE1
24 S 7	Thorburn sq SE1
8 B 11	Thoresby st N1
21 J 19	Thorncroft st SW8

19 B 18   Thorndike clo SW10
21 L 20   Thorne rd SW8
21 J 6   Thorney st SW1
9 A 17   Thornfield rd W12
2 V 17   Thorngate rd W9
5 H 19   Thornhaugh st WC1
6 O 7   Thornhill br N1
6 O 1   Thornhill cres N1
6 R 2   Thornhill gro N1
6 S 2   Thornhill rd N1
6 O 2   Thornhill sq N1
19 H 19   Thornley cres SW11
21 G 20   Thorparch rd SW8
9 M 4   Thorpe ms W10
15 C 14   Thrale st SE1
15 G 6   Threadneedle sy EC2
8 Y 16   Three Colts la E2
12 W 8   Three Kings yd W1
16 N 17   Three Oak la SE1
12 E 16   Three Tuns ct SE1
9 J 9   Threshers pl W11
15 G 5   Throgmorton st EC2
22 Z 9   Thrush st SE17
24 S 1   Thurland rd SE16
19 J 4   Thurloe clo SW7
19 G 4   Thurloe Pl ms SW7
19 H 4   Thurloe pl SW7
19 H 5   Thurloe sq SW7
19 G 5   Thurloe st SW7
23 H 10   Thurlow st SE17
8 O 7   Thurtle rd E2
7 A 2   Tibberton sq N1
11 K 6   Tichbourne row W2
8 T 12   Tillett way E2
16 X 7   Tillman st E1
6 N 2   Tilloch st N1
7 C 16   Tilney ct EC1
12 U 13   Tilney st W1
17 M 15   Tilton st SW6
7 A 17   Timber st EC1
16 Y 6   Timberland rd E1
22 X 20   Tindal st SW9
21 M 8   Tinworth st SE11
22 N 9   Tinworth st SE11
13 E 9   Tisbury ct W1
23 G 8   Tisdall pl SE17
3 M 7   Titchfield rd NW8
4 N 7   Titchfield rd NW8
20 P 13   Tite st SW3
1 H 6   Tiverton rd NW10
23 A 2   Tiverton st SE1
2 W 8   Tollgate gdns NW6
5 C 15   Tolmers sq NW1
8 P 1   Tomlinson clo E2
6 X 14   Tompion st EC1
5 J 12   Tonbridge st WC1
14 S 4   Tooks ct EC4
15 K 15   Tooley st SE1
16 N 18   Tooley st SE1
22 R 5   Topaz st SE11
6 S 17   Topham st EC1
10 U 16   Tor gdns W8
2 O 2   Torbay rd NW6
10 W 2   Torquay St W2
6 V 9   Torrens st N1
5 D 19   Torrington pl WC1
13 G 20   Tothill st SW1
5 C 18   Tottenham Court rd W1
13 F 2   Tottenham Court rd W1
13 C 1   Tottenham ms W1
13 C 1   Tottenham st W1
15 A 18   Toulmin st SE1
23 A 18   Toulon st SE5
18 R 17   Tournay rd SW6
16 O 11   Tower Br appr E1
16 N 14   Tower br E1
15 M 18   Tower Br rd SE1
23 J 3   Tower Br rd SE1
13 H 7   Tower ct WC2
15 L 10   Tower hill EC3

16 N 10   Tower hill EC3
15 M 11   Tower of London EC3
15 L 10   Tower pl EC3
13 H 7   Tower st WC2
23 D 8   Townley st SE17
23 H 6   Townsend st SE17
3 L 8   Townshend rd NW8
16 N 3   Toynbee st E1
22 S 7   Tracey st SE11
21 M 20   Tradescant rd SW8
24 O 11   Trafalgar av SE15
13 H 12   Trafalgar sq SW1
13 H 12   Trafalgar sq WC2
23 F 10   Trafalgar st SE17
11 K 2   Transept st NW1
9 H 9   Treadgold st W11
8 W 9   Treadway st E2
5 M 6   Treaty st N1
12 X 14   Trebeck st W1
18 U 9   Trebovir rd SW5
8 U 3   Trederwen rd E8
20 R 16   Tree wlk SW11
19 A 12   Tregunter rd SW10
21 K 16   Trenchold st SW8
17 M 8   Trevanion rd W14
1 C 5   Trevelyan gdns NW10
14 X 14   Treveris st SE1
1 J 19   Treverton st W10
11 M 20   Trevor pl SW7
11 M 20   Trevor sq SW7
12 N 19   Trevor sq SW7
11 M 19   Trevor st SW7
8 W 3   Triangle rd E8
22 P 16   Trigon rd SW8
15 C 20   Trinity Church sq SE1
15 M 9   Trinity sq EC3
15 C 20   Trinity st SE1
15 C 20   Trio pl SE1
5 A 16   Triton sq NW1
24 T 6   Trothy rd SE1
15 A 17   Trundle st SE1
17 B 2   Trussley rd W6
20 N 9   Tryon st SW3
8 Z 2   Tudor gro E9
13 F 3   Tudor pl W1
8 Y 3   Tudor rd E9
14 U 8   Tudor st EC4
21 H 2   Tufton st SW1
8 S 9   Tuilerie st E2
9 A 14   Tunis rd W12
8 S 14   Turin st E2
6 W 19   Turks Head yd EC1
20 R 9   Turks row SW3
14 W 4   Turnagain la EC4
16 W 4   Turner st E1
18 O 13   Turneville rd W14
18 O 13   Turney rd W14
6 V 19   Turnmill st EC1
20 X 10   Turpentine la SW1
23 C 8   Turquand st SE17
14 R 8   Tweezers all WC2
14 N 4   Twyford pl WC2
6 N 4   Twyford st N1
15 J 18   Tyers gate SE1
2 O 8   Tyers st SE11
22 O 10   Tyers ter SE11
6 T 15   Tysoe st EC1

U

21 D 6   Udall st SW1
14 W 17   Ufford st SE1
7 H 2   Ufton rd N1
4 W 18   Ulster pl NW1
4 V 18   Ulster ter NW1
16 V 5   Umberton st E1
4 Z 5   Underhill pas NW1
4 Z 5   Underhill st NW1

15 J 6   Undershaft EC3
8 S 19   Underwood rd E1
7 D 11   Underwood st N1
15 L 15   Unicorn pas SE1
7 B 6   Union sq N1
14 X 16   Union st SE1
15 A 15   Union st SE1
7 M 11   Union wlk E2
5 E 17   University college WC1
5 H 20   University of London WC1
5 C 18   University st WC1
24 R 16   Unwin rd SE15
11 D 7   Upbrook ms W2
19 C 19   Upcerne rd SW10
23 L 10   Upnor way SE17
9 J 17   Upper Addison gdns W14
20 V 1   Upper Belgrave st SW1
12 P 5   Upper Berkeley st W1
12 S 9   Upper Brook st W1
19 K 14   Upper Cheyne row SW3
12 T 10   Upper Grosvenor st W1
14 S 13   Upper ground SE1
14 V 12   Upper ground SE1
4 U 17   Upper Harley st NW1
13 C 8   Upper James st W1
13 C 9   Upper John st W1
14 P 20   Upper Marsh SE1
12 O 1   Upper Montagu st W1
10 T 19   Upper Phillimore gdns W8
13 J 8   Upper St Martins la WC2
6 W 2   Upper st N1
6 V 8   Upper st N1
14 Z 8   Upper Thames st EC4
15 B 9   Upper Thames st EC4
4 V 20   Upper Wimpole st W1
5 G 15   Upper Woburn pl WC1
23 B 16   Urlwin st SE5
19 B 18   Uverdale rd SW10
9 B 16   Uxbridge rd W12
10 S 13   Uxbridge st W8

V

3 B 13   Vale clo W9
5 J 1   Vale Royal N7
19 G 14   Vale the SW3
14 V 18   Valentine pl SE1
14 W 18   Valentine row SE1
16 U 1   Vallance rd E1
8 U 14   Vallance rd E2
13 D 20   Vandon pas SW1
21 D 1   Vandon st SW1
21 D 5   Vane st SW1
18 U 18   Vanston pl SW6
24 Z 12   Varcoe rd SE16
16 W 3   Varden st E1
5 A 2   Varndell st NW1
22 V 20   Vassall rd SW9
24 P 3   Vauban st SE16
21 C 6   Vauxhall Br rd SW1
21 J 10   Vauxhall br SW1 & SE11
21 M 13   Vauxhall gro SW8
22 N 13   Vauxhall gro SW8
21 M 15   Vauxhall pk SE11
22 P 8   Vauxhall st SE11

21 L 13 Vauxhall stn SE1
22 N 8   Vauxhall wlk SE11
21 M 10 Vauxhall wlk SE11
3 H 19   Venables st NW8
12 X 6   Vere st W1
18 N 12 Vereker rd W14
9 J 7   Verity clo W11
24 V 12 Verney rd SE16
24 V 11 Verney way SE16
17 L 6   Vernon ms W14
13 L 2   Vernon pl WC1
6 P 12   Vernon ri WC1
6 O 11   Vernon sq WC1
17 L 6   Vernon st W14
6 S 20   Verulam st EC1
7 F 12   Vestry st N1
14 V 2   Viaduct bldgs EC1
8 W 14   Viaduct pl E2
8 W 14   Viaduct st E2
5 L 4   Vibart wk N1
10 W 16 Vicarage ga W8
10 W 15 Vicarage gdns W8
8 Z 5   Vicars clo E9
21 J 7   Vickers bldg SW1
19 H 3   Victoria & Albert
          museum SW7
15 K 2   Victoria av EC2
13 L 16 Victoria emb EC4,
          WC2 & SW1
14 S 9   Victoria emb EC4,
          WC2 & SW1
10 S 12 Victoria gdns W11
10 V 10 Victoria Gro ms W2
19 A 1   Victoria gro W8
2 S 4   Victoria ms NW6
8 Y 5   Victoria Pk rd E9
8 Z 11   Victoria Pk sq E2
2 O 8   Victoria rd NW6
2 T 4   Victoria rd NW6
11 A 19 Victoria rd W8
20 Y 1   Victoria sq SW1
13 G 20 Victoria st SW1
21 D 2   Victoria st SW1
20 Y 5   Victoria stn SW1
21 K 1   Victoria Tower
          gdns SW1
23 D 5   Victory pl SE17
23 G 17 Victory sq SE5
13 B 10 Vigo st W1
23 G 12 Villa st SE17
23 F 10 Villa st SE17
13 K 12 Villiers st WC2
7 G 14   Vince st EC1
21 E 5   Vincent sq SW1
21 F 6   Vincent st SW1
6 X 9   Vincent ter N1
16 U 2   Vine ct E1
6 S 18   Vine hill EC1
15 L 15 Vine la SE1
16 N 7   Vine st EC3
13 C 11 Vine st W1
15 B 18 Vine yd SE1
3 K 14   Vinery vlls NW8
6 T 16   Vineyard wlk EC1
3 B 10   Violet hill NW8
12 N 1   Virgil pl W1
22 R 1   Virgil st SE1
7 M 14   Virginia rd E2
16 T 10 Virginia st E1
7 B 19   Viscount st EC1
8 U 14   Voss st E2
8 Y 7   Vyner st E2

W

23 D 7   Wadding st SE17
8 Y 7   Wadeson st E2
3 J 2   Wadham gdns NW3
24 O 13 Waite st SE15
5 L 15   Wakefield st WC1
1 D 13   Wakeman rd NW10

6 X 11   Wakley st EC1
21 M 19 Walberswick st SW8
16 W 7   Walburgh st E1
23 C 8   Walcorde av SE17
22 U 4   Walcot sq SE11
21 D 5   Walcott st SW1
16 V 3   Walden st E1
19 H 14 Waldron ms SW3
18 X 19 Walham Grn ct SW6
18 U 17 Walham gro SW6
18 T 16 Walham yd SW6
13 E 8   Walkers ct W1
12 T 4   Wallace collection
          W2
18 W 6   Wallgrave rd SW5
9 E 4   Wallingford av W10
12 N 1   Walmer pl W1
9 J 9   Walmer rd W11
9 K 9   Walmer rd W11
12 N 1   Walmer st W1
22 S 4   Walnut Tree wlk
          SE11
20 O 9   Walpole st SW3
2 R 17   Walterton rd W9
21 L 17 Walton clo SW3
20 O 1   Walton pl SW3
19 L 5   Walton st SW3
20 N 3   Walton st SW3
23 C 10 Walworth pl SE17
23 B 9   Walworth rd SE17
18 Z 18 Wandon rd SW6
21 H 18 Wandsworth rd SW8
18 W 18 Wansdown pl SW6
23 B 7   Wansey st SE17
16 Z 14 Wapping Dock st E1
16 T 14 Wapping High st E1
16 X 10 Wapping la E1
8 X 3   Warburton rd E8
22 P 8   Ward st SE11
15 A 15 Wardens gro SE1
13 D 6   Wardour ms W1
13 E 7   Wardour st W1
14 Y 7   Wardrobe pl EC4
14 Y 7   Wardrobe ter EC4
1 F 14   Warfield rd NW10
1 F 14   Warfield yd NW10
22 X 18 Warham st SE5
2 R 16   Warlock rd W9
8 Y 4   Warneford st E9
8 T 10   Warner pl E2
6 R 17   Warner st EC1
6 S 18   Warner yd EC1
4 Z 18   Warren ms W1
5 B 17   Warren st W1
3 A 17   Warrington cres W9
3 A 19   Warrington gdns W9
2 Y 17   Warwick av W9
3 A 19   Warwick av W9
11 B 1   Warwick cres W2
14 R 2   Warwick ct WC1
18 P 3   Warwick gdns W14
13 F 13 Warwick Ho st SW1
14 Y 5   Warwick la EC4
2 Z 18   Warwick ms W9
20 Z 8   Warwick Pl north
          SW1
3 A 20   Warwick pl W9
18 T 8   Warwick rd SW5
18 P 5   Warwick rd W14
20 Z 2   Warwick row SW1
21 A 1   Warwick row SW1
14 Y 5   Warwick sq EC4
21 A 8   Warwick Sq ms SW1
21 A 8   Warwick sq SW1
13 C 9   Warwick st W1
20 X 9   Warwick way SW1
21 B 6   Warwick way SW1
14 R 8   Water st WC2
14 W 8   Watergate EC4
13 L 12 Watergate wlk WC2
17 H 8   Waterhouse clo W6
14 O 11 Waterloo br WC2
2 R 1   Waterloo pas NW6

13 F 13 Waterloo pl SW1
14 U 18 Waterloo rd SE1
14 R 16 Waterloo stn SE1
6 W 2   Waterloo ter N1
16 T 19 Waterside clo SE16
4 U 3   Waterside pl NW1
7 L 12   Waterson st N1
15 B 7   Watling st EC4
16 Y 6   Watney mkt E1
16 R 18 Watney pas SE1
16 Y 8   Watney st E1
16 X 13 Watts st E1
2 W 2   Wavel ms NW6
3 F 8   Waverley pl NW8
12 V 12 Waverton st W1
14 P 20 Waxwell ter SE1
9 F 7   Wayneflete sq W10
8 W 13   Wear pl E2
8 S 18   Weaver st E1
15 L 15 Weavers la SE1
23 J 3   Webb st SE1
14 V 19 Webber row SE1
14 X 18 Webber st SE1
24 U 2   Webster rd SE16
1 M 17   Wedlake st W10
16 T 5   Wehill rd E1
12 V 7   Weighhouse st W1
5 G 13   Weirs pas NW1
12 W 5   Welbeck st W1
12 W 4   Welbeck way W1
8 Z 1   Well st E9
16 T 8   Wellclose sq E1
16 T 10 Wellclose st E1
15 A 17 Weller st SE1
5 J 10   Wellers ct NW1
7 C 12   Wellesley ter N1
10 S 6   Wellington clo W11
3 H 12   Wellington pl NW8
1 G 14   Wellington rd NW10
3 G 10   Wellington rd NW8
8 R 12   Wellington row E2
20 N 10 Wellington sq SW3
13 M 8   Wellington st WC2
14 N 8   Wellington st WC2
10 W 11 Wellington ter W2
12 P 2   Wells Ms W1
9 C 19   Wells rd W12
4 O 6   Wells ri NW8
13 B 3   Wells st W1
23 H 16 Wells way SE5
24 S 8   Welsford st SE1
8 U 4   Welshpool st E8
7 B 10   Wenlock rd N1
7 D 10   Wenlock st N1
24 P 20 Wentworth cres
          SE15
16 P 3   Wentworth st E1
5 D 10   Werrington st NW1
22 X 8   Wesley clo SE17
12 V 1   Wesley st W1
13 K 4   West Central st
          WC1
18 T 6   West Cromwell rd
          SW5
20 S 4   West Eaton Pl ms
          SW1
20 S 4   West Eaton pl SW1
2 V 4   West End la NW6
16 Z 10 West gdns E1
20 S 1   West Halkin st SW1
14 T 5   West Harding st
          EC4
16 W 19 West la SE16
10 V 12 West mall W8
20 Z 8   West ms SW1
14 W 2   West Poultry av
          EC1
1 J 17   West row W10
14 X 2   West Smithfield
          EC1
22 W 3   West sq SE11
13 H 7   West st WC2
16 O 7   West Tenter st E1

20 Z 8 West Warwick pl SW1
11 E 8 Westbourne cres W2
10 X 4 Westbourne gdns W2
10 T 7 Westbourne Gro ms W11
10 X 5 Westbourne Gro ter W2
10 W 6 Westbourne gro W2
10 X 5 Westbourne Pk ms W2
10 X 4 Westbourne Pk rd W2
10 R 4 Westbourne Pk rd W11
10 W 3 Westbourne Pk vlls W2
11 G 9 Westbourne st W2
11 C 5 Westbourne Ter ms W2
11 A 1 Westbourne Ter rd W2
11 A 3 Westbourne ter W2
19 J 20 Westbridge rd SW11
22 X 12 Westcott rd SE17
10 S 1 Western Av extn W2
2 R 19 Western ms W9
8 X 3 Westgate st E8
18 Y 12 Westgate ter SW10
22 Z 19 Westhall rd SE5
7 D 12 Westland pl N1
21 B 3 Westminster Cathedral SW1
13 J 20 Westminster Abbey SW1
14 P 18 Westminster Br rd SE1
13 L 18 Westminster br SW1
20 Y 11 Westmoreland pl SW1
12 V 1 Westmoreland st W1
20 Y 10 Westmoreland ter SW1
6 O 11 Weston ri WC1
15 H 17 Weston st SE1
8 Z 1 Weston wlk E9
9 B 7 Westway W12
9 E 19 Westwick gdns W14
19 A 8 Wetherby gdns SW5
18 Y 9 Wetherby ms SW5
19 B 7 Wetherby pl SW7
12 X 1 Weymouth ms W1
12 X 1 Weymouth ms W1
8 O 8 Weymouth pl E2
4 X 20 Weymouth st W1
12 W 1 Weymouth st W1
8 O 9 Weymouth ter E2
8 U 7 Wharf pl E2
7 B 11 Wharf rd N1
7 A 9 Wharf rd N1
5 L 8 Wharfedale rd N1
18 X 11 Wharfedale st SW10
6 R 13 Wharton cotts WC1
6 P 13 Wharton st WC1
12 V 1 Wheatley st W1
17 E 18 Wheatsheaf la SW6
21 K 17 Wheatsheaf la SW8
18 R 20 Wheatsheaf ter SW6
1 L 20 Wheatstone rd W10
5 K 4 Wheeler gdns N1
8 N 18 Wheler st E1
14 O 3 Whetstone pk WC2
5 K 13 Whidborne st WC1
6 V 14 Whiskin st EC1
19 H 20 Whistless av SW11
8 S 6 Whiston rd E2
7 M 7 Whiston rd E2
8 N 16 Whitby st E1
9 G 9 Whitchurch rd W11
13 G 11 Whitcomb st WC2
6 T 19 White Bear yd EC1
16 S 4 White Ch la E1
9 B 9 White City clo W12

9 A 9 White City rd W12
9 B 9 White City Stadium W10
6 T 7 White Conduit st N1
15 J 3 White Hart ct EC2
22 V 9 White Hart st SE11
15 F 15 White Hart yd SE1
12 Y 14 White Horse st W1
15 M 4 White Kennett st E1
14 Z 9 White Lion hill EC4
6 S 9 White Lion st N1
12 X 8 White Lion yd W1
16 R 3 Whitechapel High st E1
8 X 20 Whitechapel rd E1
16 U 2 Whitechapel rd E1
7 H 20 Whitecross pl EC2
7 C 17 Whitecross st EC1
7 C 17 Whitecross st EC1
14 U 6 Whitefriars st EC4
13 K 14 Whitehall ct SW1
13 K 15 Whitehall gdns SW1
13 K 13 Whitehall pl SW1
13 J 15 Whitehall SW1
3 J 19 Whitehaven st NW8
19 M 8 Whiteheads gro SW3
15 L 17 Whites grounds SE1
16 N 2 Whites row E1
5 B 18 Whitfield pl W1
5 B 18 Whitfield st W1
13 D 1 Whitfield st W1
22 N 6 Whitgift st SE11
1 C 8 Whitmore gdns NW10
20 S 7 Whittaker st SW1
15 J 7 Whittington av EC3
14 T 15 Whittlesey st SE1
16 V 7 Wicker st E1
8 Z 17 Wickford st E1
22 O 9 Wickham st SE11
6 N 12 Wicklow st WC1
5 M 12 Wicklow st WC1
15 L 2 Widegate st E1
2 V 15 Widley rd W9
12 X 4 Wigmore pl W1
12 W 4 Wigmore st W1
22 T 11 Wigton pl SE1
20 R 5 Wilbraham pl SW1
10 P 12 Wilby ms W11
1 K 19 Wilcox clo SW8
21 J 18 Wilcox rd SW8
13 M 5 Wild ct WC2
13 M 6 Wild st WC2
8 T 4 Wilde clo E8
15 H 20 Wilds rents SE1
23 H 1 Wilds rents SE1
21 B 1 Wilfred st SW1
8 P 18 Wilkes st E1
16 O 1 Wilkes st E1
22 N 20 Wilkinson st SW8
7 K 9 Wilks pl N1
1 M 1 Willesden la NW6 & NW2
2 R 2 Willesden la NW6 & NW2
24 W 11 Willet way SE16
24 X 11 Willet way SE16
13 J 11 William IV st WC2
12 R 18 William ms SW1
4 Z 14 William rd NW1
5 A 15 William rd NW1
12 R 18 William st SW1
13 H 2 Willoughby st WC1
21 C 5 Willow pl SW1
7 H 15 Willow st EC2
23 L 5 Willow wlk SE1
24 N 6 Willow wlk SE1
24 P 17 Willowbrook rd SE15
7 K 6 Wilmer gdns N1
6 S 15 Wilmington sq WC1

6 S 14 Wilmington st WC1
24 S 20 Wilmot clo SE15
8 X 14 Wilmot st E2
9 J 12 Wilsham st W11
16 V 19 Wilson gro SE16
15 G 1 Wilson st EC2
7 G 19 Wilson st EC2
12 S 19 Wilton cres SW1
20 V 1 Wilton ms SW1
12 S 18 Wilton pl SW1
12 T 19 Wilton row SW1
7 E 4 Wilton sq N1
20 W 1 Wilton st SW1
12 T 20 Wilton ter SW1
7 D 4 Wilton vlls N1
8 S 11 Wimbolt st E2
7 E 8 Wimbourne st N1
12 W 1 Wimpole ms W1
12 W 2 Wimpole st W1
1 M 2 Winchester av NW6
22 Y 7 Winchester clo SE17
3 H 1 Winchester rd NW3
15 E 12 Winchester sq SE1
21 A 10 Winchester st SW1
20 Y 9 Winchester st SW1
15 E 13 Winchester wlk SE1
22 T 6 Wincott st SE11
1 M 6 Windermere ms NW6
22 S 11 Windmill row SE11
13 E 2 Windmill st W1
14 U 16 Windmill wlk SE1
21 C 4 Windsor pl SW1
6 Y 4 Windsor st N1
16 Z 11 Wine clo E1
14 V 5 Wine Office ct EC4
17 E 15 Wingrave rd W6
13 E 8 Winnett st W1
7 B 11 Winsdor ter N1
11 G 5 Winslade ms W2
11 F 4 Winsland st W2
13 B 4 Winsley st W1
17 E 12 Winslow rd W6
19 D 13 Winterton pl SW10
8 W 20 Winthrop st E1
8 Y 15 Witan st E2
24 X 10 Witherfield way SE16
24 X 11 Witherfield way SE16
5 H 17 Woburn pl WC1
5 G 18 Woburn sq WC1
5 G 15 Woburn wlk WC1
16 R 18 Wolseley st SE1
16 Z 1 Wolsey st E1
17 E 6 Wolverton gdns W6
8 S 16 Wood clo E2
9 C 10 Wood la W12
15 C 2 Wood st EC2
6 V 16 Woodbridge st EC1
2 X 20 Woodchester sq W2
2 W 1 Woodchurch rd NW6
20 O 10 Woodfall St SW3
2 S 19 Woodfield pl W9
2 R 20 Woodfield rd W9
9 M 17 Woodford sq W14
6 C 19 Woodger rd W6
17 F 19 Woodlawn rd SW6
9 A 2 Woodmans ms W10
12 S 9 Woods ms W1
23 K 2 Woods pl SE1
8 R 20 Woodseer st E1
9 H 18 Woodstock gro W12
12 V 1 Woodstock ms W1
12 X 7 Woodstock st W1
2 R 8 Woodville rd NW6
23 F 10 Wooler st SE17
24 R 4 Woolstaplers way SE16
14 U 15 Wootton st SE1
19 M 19 Worfield st SW11
22 N 9 Worgan st SE11
7 G 8 Worgate st N1

17 C 10 Worlidge st W6
15 H 3 Wormwood st EC2
1 M 19 Wornington rd W10
1 K 18 Wornington rd W10
10 N 1 Wornington rd W10
3 H 5 Woronzow rd NW8
7 G 19 Worship st EC2
6 O 16 Wren st WC1
1 F 7 Wrentham av NW10
18 W 1 Wrights la W8
10 W 20 Wrights la W8
5 C 1 Wrotham rd NW1
6 W 14 Wyclif st EC1
17 L 20 Wyfold rd SW6
2 V 14 Wymering rd W9
12 O 2 Wyndham ms W1
12 O 2 Wyndham pl W1
23 B 19 Wyndham rd SE5
22 Z 19 Wyndham rd SE5
12 O 1 Wyndham st W1

6 R 8 Wynford rd N1
6 O 8 Wynford rd N1
18 U 1 Wynnstay gdns W8
22 R 10 Wynyard ter SE11
6 W 12 Wynyatt st EC1
12 O 5 Wythburn pl W1
21 J 17 Wyvil est SW8
21 K 16 Wyvil rd SW8

Y

24 R 5 Yalding rd SE16
6 S 14 Yardley st WC1
12 X 14 Yarmouth pl W1
7 E 1 Yeate st N1
17 E 10 Yeldham rd W6
19 L 3 Yeomans row SW3

16 R 8 Yeomans yd E1
23 B 9 York av SE17
13 L 11 York bldgs WC2
4 U 18 York ga NW1
10 X 17 York Ho pl W8
13 K 11 York pl WC2
14 P 16 York rd SE1
12 R 1 York st W1
4 U 18 York Ter east NW1
4 T 18 York Ter west NW1
5 K 4 York way N1
8 R 9 Yorkton st E2
10 Y 19 Young st W8

Z

15 A 13 Zoar st SE1